Body and Soul

POETS ON POETRY

David Lehman, General Editor
Donald Hall, Founding Editor

Mark Jarman

Body and Soul

ESSAYS ON POETRY

Ann Arbor

THE UNIVERSITY OF MICHIGAN PRESS

2005   2004   2003   2002   4   3   2   1

A CIP catalog record for this book is available from the British Library.

Library of Congress Cataloging-in-Publication Data

Jarman, Mark.
     Body and soul : essays on poetry / Mark Jarman.
        p.   cm. — (Poets on poetry)
     ISBN 0-472-09802-0 (Cloth : alk. paper) – ISBN 0-472-06802-4
(Paper : alk. paper)
     1. Jarman, Mark—Aesthetics.   2. Poetry.   I. Title.   II. Series.
PS3560 .A537 B63 2002
809 .1—dc21   2002000565

To the memory of Donald Davie

Acknowledgments

Grateful acknowledgment is made for permission to reprint the following:

"Life Encompassed" by Donald Davie. From *Collected Poems* by Donald Davie. Copyright 1991 by Donald Davie. Reprinted by permission of University of Chicago Press.

"Tor House" by Robinson Jeffers. From *The Selected Poetry of Robinson Jeffers* by Robinson Jeffers. Copyright 1923 & renewed 1956 by Robinson Jeffers. Reprinted by permission of Random House, Inc.

"Landscape, Dense with Trees" by Ellen Bryant Voigt. From *The Lotus Flowers* by Ellen Bryant Voigt. Copyright 1987 by Ellen Bryant Voigt. Reprinted by permission of W. W. Norton & Company, Inc.

"Shore Leave" by Lynda Hull. From *Star Ledger* by Lynda Hull. Copyright 1991 by Lynda Hull. Reprinted by permission of The University of Iowa Press.

"Yellow Light" by Garrett Kaoru Hongo. From *Yellow Light* by Garrett Kaoru Hongo. Copyright 1982 by Garrett Kaoru Hongo. Reprinted by permission of University Press of New England.

"Test Pilot" by Robert McDowell. From *At the House of the Tin Man* by Robert McDowell. Copyright 1983 by Robert McDowell. Reprinted by permission of the author.

"Directive" by Robert Frost. From *The Poetry of Robert Frost,* edited by Edward Connery Lathem. Copyright 1969 by Henry Holt and Company, LLC. Reprinted by permission of Henry Holt & Co., LLC.

"Slip, Shift, and Speed Up: The Influence of Robinson Jeffers' Narrative Syntax." From *Jeffers Studies,* Fall 1999, V. 3, N. 4.

"'Out, Out—'" by Robert Frost. From *The Poetry of Robert Frost,* edited by Edward Connery Lathem. Copyright 1969 by Henry Holt and Company, LLC. Reprinted by permission of Henry Holt & Co., LLC.

Contents

Preface

Remembering D. D.

This book is dedicated to the memory of Donald Davie, my colleague at Vanderbilt University from 1983, when I came to teach there, until 1987, when he retired and returned to his home in England. As a poet, he began his career in the 1950s as part of The Movement, a loosely associated group of English formalists, including Philip Larkin and Thom Gunn, who reacted against the excesses of Modernism. As a critic, he was divided in his interests, for besides being the most articulate spokesman for The Movement, he also became one of the major authorities on Ezra Pound and maintained a lifelong curiosity in American poetry of the Pound tradition. As a colleague, he loved debate over intellectual issues, especially about poetry. Between the two of us, the debate concerned the importance of narrative in poetry—my issue—and the importance of the New Formalism—his.

I have no doubt that I was hired to teach at Vanderbilt with Donald Davie's approval, even though my coeditor, Robert McDowell, and I had criticized him in the first issue of our magazine, *The Reaper.* In 1979 Davie had taken part in a literary symposium called "After the Flood" at the Folger Shakespeare Library in Washington, D.C., and there he had argued for greater formality in contemporary poetry and less emphasis on the personal. McDowell and I wrote a critique of the symposium in which we disagreed with everything that had been said, even Davie's comments, which we would come to endorse, and caricatured him as an old-fashioned schoolmaster. When I met Davie for the first time at my job interview at Vanderbilt and he made no mention of the critical essay, though we had sent him a copy of the magazine, I thought he must not have seen or read it. The first day we were both at school he invited me to his office. I sat down across from him at his desk, and he showed me that he did indeed have a copy of the first issue of *The Reaper*, which contained our essay. He said that it had made him angry when he read it three years previously and still made him angry. He believed that, at the symposium, he had been proposing a countermeasure to the current fashions of poetry, just as McDowell and I were in our little magazine. At that meeting, as I sat amazed, for I knew I had been forgiven for what I had written, Davie and I began a debate about the role of traditional English verse in contemporary American poetry which we continued until he retired and for some years afterward. Before he died in 1995, I had been persuaded to his point of view, that far from being obsolete and inaccurate measures of American speech and life, the traditional forms and meters of English verse offer continued vitality. They are evergreen. And it is foolish to exclude them as valid modes of expression.

Davie maintained a belief in the poem as a made thing, an object of meaning that radiates meaning through all its parts, something with weight—moral weight, indeed, for which a poet should feel responsible as its maker. In other words, a poem has an essential value created by its author, and this value is reflected in the workmanship of the poem, which can be judged practically, as he would say, as good or less good. Though Davie often referred to himself as a practical critic, I suspect that his attitude toward poetry was related to his religious faith. Reading his essays in *A Gathered Church*, his preface to *The Oxford Book of Christian Verse*, which he had edited, and his account of his baptism in the Anglican church in his memoir *These the Companions* and following the thread of religious concerns in his poetry, culminating in his last collection, *To Scorch or Freeze: Poems About the Sacred*, I realized Davie's religious life was intimately involved with his poetry. This realization was part of what led me to engage my own religious beliefs more directly in my writing.

Finally, the example of Donald Davie as a poet and critic struck me particularly because I saw that he could change his mind, that he could learn to appreciate what had previously seemed beneath his notice. Though he could not share it, he understood my admiration for William Carlos Williams, and I believe our conversations about narrative poetry led him to look more closely at Robinson Jeffers. He appeared to be actively engaged in looking and looking again, while aware that one would never be able to comprehend everything. The poem of his I find myself most often repeating is "Life Encompassed," from his book *Events and Wisdoms:*

> How often I have said,
> "This will never do,"
> Of ways of feeling that now
> I trust in, and pursue!
>
> Do traverses tramped in the past,
> My own, criss-crossed as I forge
> Across from another quarter
> Speak of a life encompassed?
>
> Well, life is not research.
> No one asks you to map the terrain,
> Only to get across it
> In new ways, time and again.
>
> How many such, even now,
> I dismiss out of hand
> As not to my purpose, not
> Unknown, just unexamined.[1]

This poem reminds me of the limitations of critical understanding and opinion, and also of the importance and necessity of growth in the life of the mind.

I can only say that I am grateful for Donald Davie's influence and hopeful that it is reflected in the essays and reviews gathered here.

NOTE

1. From *Collected Poems* by Donald Davie. Reprinted by permission of the University of Chicago Press.

The Body on Fire, the Soul in Flight

We cannot know the soul without the body. Not only great re-
ligious poetry, but all great poetry teaches us this truth.
Whether the body is the one of an artist who considers himself
ugly and warped by his work or it is the body of an imprisoned
monk, still this radiant node of the senses is where God is ap-
prehended, if one is looking for God, and where the soul,
which connects us to God, takes the shape of imagination. In
his poetry, Michelangelo carves a soul from the passions of the
flesh, often employing Petrarchan conventions of fire and ice
as the chisels. St. John of the Cross, in response to his im-
prisonment, sees his soul escaping in his poetry, in flight as an-
other body, a bird's or a deer's, taking his lead from the author
of "Song of Songs." Both poets write to capture God's atten-
tion, speaking as if to a lover. In his love poems for other
people, men and women, Michelangelo speaks with the same
emotion that imbues his poems for God; there is little differ-
ence between them. Consistently he sees his physical appear-
ance as evidence of a fall from grace, but intuits salvation
through his artistic gifts. He is a more personal poet than St.
John of the Cross, and we can trace events in his life through
the poems and fragments he left behind. But St. John of the
Cross gives us poems with a satisfying intellectual sense of com-
pletion, due in part to his enjoyment of paradox. His poetry is
less tortured than Michelangelo's, possibly because the monk
saw the contradiction in believing the soul was the body's pris-
oner, rather than its mate.

Review of *The Complete Poems of Michelangelo* (John Frederick Nims,
translator) and *The Poems of St. John of the Cross* (Ken Krabbenhoft, trans-
lator), from *The Kenyon Review* (summer/fall 2001).

The subject of a religious poem is clear; it is the real or imagined tie between the poet and God. The urgency with which the poet tries to understand that tie gives religious poetry its power. John Donne fearing for his immortal soul, Gerard Manley Hopkins pleading for divine help—these are obvious examples of why such poetry exists and continues to move us as readers. Whether or not we share the beliefs of these poets, we feel what moves them to write. In "Love (III)," George Herbert's shame and amazement at being welcomed and waited upon by Love itself give us a poignant drama. We all understand how it feels to be grateful for something we do not deserve, to feel gratitude for mercy, whether or not we believe mercy is God-given.

It is very likely that the greatest religious poetry of the European tradition occurred during the Renaissance because of the growth of humanism. Rediscovering the classical emphasis on the human meant recognizing a new relationship between the human and the divine. It meant seeing the divine first in the human, which led to a new glorification and realism in dealing with the body but aroused a troubling responsibility. From this responsibility eventually came alienation and existential courage. But first there was the trouble of recognizing that the God in humanity might be less than the God in heaven, and, in fact, that locating God in the human might paradoxically create a new distance between God and creation. Humanity was alone with its new divinity. Religious poetry during the Renaissance reflects a fear and wonder at a paradoxical, new universe that centered on Leonardo's spread-eagled human figure. Like the other great religious poets of the Renaissance, Michelangelo and St. John of the Cross felt this wonder and fear and responsibility as dimensions of the soul. They felt it in their flesh and blood and in their bones.

Despite his artistic genius, Michelangelo is, for the most part, a conventional poet of his time. And as such, he expresses himself in the conventions of Petrarch. The give and take between lovers occurs through the eyes and the heart:

> If your pitiless arrows missed by far
> the target of my heart, long years ago,
> revenge is yours; your eyes, so dazzling, throw
> far deadlier darts my way, none going wide. (9)

Yet because of his practice as a sculptor, he is also able to employ the ice and fire of Petrarch in dynamic ways:

> No ordeal lasts when age begins to tell.
> That's why I seem like ice the flames enwrap:
> it shrinks, writhes to escape, but won't ignite.
> I'm old. (17)

One can see the agony of melting sculpture in that writhing ice. Elsewhere he is less original, referring to his heart as charred and advising others, "Flee from this Love, you lovers; flee the flame! / The burning's bitter . . ." (20). He sees himself especially susceptible in his age, writing in a madrigal when he was at least seventy:

> Unhappy soul, with no evasive art
> at hand those early days,
> and now on edge to dart
> and die in many a blaze
> set long ago! The one no flare could faze
> in his green age—what truth time's mirror told!—
> now the least spark consumes—decrepit, old. (127)

Poetry appears to be a medium the older Michelangelo turned to, especially as he felt himself consumed by passion for those he loved, and as he recognized a need to be reconciled with God. Because his poetry was an alternative to his true calling, its quality varies. But when he forgoes convention, he is masterful.

One reads Michelangelo's poetry hoping to see the sculptor emerge, and he does, and when he does, the poetry takes on a freshness equal to its personal urgency. The anatomist who knew the musculature of the body is present in the following passage, in which the Petrarchan eye, that symbolic weapon, comes alive with closely observed detail:

> As slowly it stirs beneath the lid, we spy
> merely a segment of its globe, and so
> the serenity of its scope is lost thereby.
> Covered, it doesn't dart much high or low;
> less lid's apparent when the eye's agape;

unfurling, it leaves few crinkles there to show.
    White's very white, black's black as a funeral drape
(if that can be) and lion-like the hue
of its fiber-to-fiber reticulated crepe. (23)

When Michelangelo makes an entire conceit of his occupation, he is capable of the wit and sexual punning of Donne, but a hundred years ahead of the English priest. All of sonnet 46 bears reading here:

> If my rough hammer shapes the obdurate stone
> to a human figure, this or that one, say,
> it's the wielder's fist, vision, and mind at play
> that gives it momentum—another's, not its own.
>   But the heavenly hammer working by God's throne
> by itself makes others and self as well. We know
> it takes a hammer to make a hammer. So
> the rest derive from that primal tool alone.
>   Since any stroke is mightier the higher
> it's launched from over the forge, one kind and wise
> has lately flown from mine to a loftier sphere.
>   My hammer is botched, unfinished in the fire
> until God's workshop help him supervise
> the tool of my craft, that alone he trued, down here. (28)

Much of Michelangelo's poetry was written in middle and old age, both extended periods for a man who lived to be nearly ninety. He was enough of a Neo-Platonist to believe that his body reflected his soul, so he suffers the onslaught not only of love but of physical decay. But even as a young man, working on the Sistine ceiling, he depicts himself with a graphic physicality that suggests an uneasy sense of his immortal part:

> A goiter it seems I got from this backward craning
> like the cats get there in Lombardy, or wherever
> —bad water, they say, from lapping their fetid river.
> My belly, tugged under my chin, 's all out of whack.
>   Beard points like a finger at heaven. Near the back
> of my neck, skull scrapes where a hunchback's hump would be.
> I'm pigeon-breasted, a harpy! Face dribbled—see?—
> like a Byzantine floor, mosaic. From all this straining

my guts and my hambones tangle, pretty near.
Thank God I can swivel my butt about for ballast.
Feet are out of sight; they just scuffle round, erratic,
      Up front my hide's tight elastic; in the rear
it's slack and droopy, except where crimps have callused.
I'm bent like a bow, half-round, type Asiatic.
      Not odd that what's on my mind,
when expressed, comes out weird, jumbled. Don't berate;
no gun with its barrel screwy can shoot straight. (10)

He is never so moving as when he writes about his own body,
thereby anatomizing and sculpting his most original poetry.
This early sonnet brackets his work with a late poem in terza
rima, completed when he was seventy-four:

      Skull hums like a hornet in a wooden pail;
gunnysack skin totes bones and jute around;
bladder's a pouch of gravel, edged like shale.
      My eyes: mauve pigment pestled till it's ground;
teeth: oboe-keys that, when I puff out air,
whistle it through or else begrudge the sound.
      My face says, "Boo!" It's scary. Rags I wear
rout—without bow and arrow—flocks of crows
from fresh-sown furrows even when weather's fair.
      One ear's all spider fuzz. I've tremolos
in the one an all-night vocal cricket chooses.
Can't sleep for my raucous snuffling, mouth and nose. (144)

One recognizes Yeats's "tattered coat upon a stick." And
Michelangelo does not spare his poetry, either:

      Amor, flower-quilted grottos, all the Muses,
for these I scribbled reams—now scraps to tot
up tabs, wrap fish, scrub toilets, or worse uses. (144)

The Renaissance individual, as we imagine him or her, is a
whole person, or at least desires to be whole, despite a begin-
ning awareness of what Eliot would call the dissociated sensibil-
ity, the existential inkling of an absent God and an individual's
terrible freedom. Michelangelo's appeals to his lord reflect the
desire for wholeness that he was able to create in his art. Early

in his career he scorned the hypocrisy of the church, and he imagined the inflamed response of Christ to contemporary Italy:

> Chalices hammered into sword and helmet!
> Christ's blood sold, slopped in palmfuls. With the yields
> from commerce of cross and thorns, more lances, shields.
> Still His long-suffering mercy falls like dew?
>
> These lands are lands He'd better not come through.
> If He did, His blood would boil, seething sky-high,
> what with his flesh on sale in good supply. (12)

As a young man, Michelangelo had heard similar things from the mouth of the fanatical Florentine reformer Savonarola. But at the end of his life, as his eyesight failed, he sounds a note we will not hear again until Gerard Manley Hopkins:

> Oh let me see You everywhere I go!
> If mortal beauty sets the soul afire,
> Your dazzle will show how dim it is; desire
> for You burns high, as once in heaven's own air. (146)

The body that he knew as intimately as any artist before or since becomes "a monstrous stone" in which he is "enclosed and hidden" (147). The last fragment of his poetry asks for release and reminds God, "You peel of flesh the same souls You appareled / in flesh . . ." (156). The paradox of Renaissance Christianity emerges from this poetry like one of the great sculptor's slaves, struggling in stone.

Michelangelo died in 1564, the year of Shakespeare's birth. Thirteen years later, in Spain, the Carmelite friar Juan de Yepes was imprisoned in Toledo by fellow Carmelite monks, who opposed the reforms of which he was part. He escaped and found refuge, first in a convent of Carmelite nuns, then in a hermitage in Andalusia, his home. During that tumultuous year, he wrote over a dozen poems which are masterpieces of religious yearning and devotion. According to the critic and translator Willis Barnstone, "From the darkness of the whale he came into the clarity and beauty of the Andalusian landscape. Here in solitude his career as a poet was fixed." Fray Juan de Yepes, who would be canonized in 1726, 135 years after his death, as St. John of the Cross, was the descendent of converted Jews. It seems fitting, then, that it is the poetry of the Old Testament, specifically "The Song of Songs," that we hear in his verse. It is also notable that his gift for paradox, his ability to contain contradictory ideas within a single image, may have reflected his own dual identity.

In "Spiritual Canticle," a bride complains that her bridegroom has fled, leaving her alone:

> Where have you hidden,
> my Love, why have you left me moaning?
> Like a stag you fled
> from having wounded me:
> I cried for you, but you were gone. (3)

And, as in "The Song of Songs," the bridegroom answers, as if it were she who had left:

> Return, my dove:
> the wounded stag, now
> bounding up the slope,
> stirs at your flight, breathing the fresh air. (7)

The pair speak to and of each other antiphonally, separated and united in a setting that recalls a medieval world of strongholds penetrated by lovers who meet in gardens, but in this case the lovers "push into the wilds more deeply" (15). They penetrate the landscape of St. John's Andalusia:

> And then we'll go on up,
> up to the caverns of stone
> that are so high and well hidden.
> And there we will enter
> to taste wine pressed from pomegranates. (15)

Surely, he knew the thrill of escape, of flight, and he understood that the sexual excitement of lovers escaping to be alone together mirrored the paradoxical pleasure of being alone with God.

The flight of the prisoner is always a paradox, resolved because it is mental flight. St. John of the Cross actually escaped his imprisonment, but what strikes a contemporary reader is that the poet expresses his communion with the holy not only in erotic terms, but as if engaged in a secret tryst:

> In darkness and secure,
> down the secret ladder, disguised,
> O joyful chance!,
> in darkness, and shielded,
> my house lying silent at last,
>
> one joyful night,
> in secret: no one was watching
> and I saw no other thing,
> my only light and guide
> the light that burned in my heart.
>
> That same light led me
> more surely than the noonday sun
> to where one was waiting,
> the one I knew would come,
> where surely no one would find us. (19)

Desire for anything, including closeness with God, cannot be expressed except in terms of the body's longing, and gratification of desire cannot be expressed except in the same way. Yet throughout his poetry, St. John of the Cross also speaks of elevation, an upward flight:

> Longing for a love affair
> in hope of love I did not delay
> but flew up so high in the air
> that I caught up with the prey.
>
> In order to catch up
> to that divine affair,
> I had to fly so high
> I flew straight out of sight. (37)

Such spiritual aspiration is part of the paradox: for the body does not have wings, though the mind does. The desire for transcendence is also bound up with erotic longing. Although the poet may claim, "My soul is unattached / to any created thing" (51), yet Love

> turns into my delight
> making my soul like itself.
> And so, in the delightful flame
> that I feel within myself,
> swiftly and thoroughly
> I consume myself completely. (51)

It is possible, too, that St. John of the Cross was comfortable with paradox because he believed in the paradox of the incarnation. He could imagine intangible and ineffable concepts alive in flesh and blood:

> God, lying in the crib,
> cried out loud and groaned
> . . . .
> And his Mother was aghast
> to see this transformation:
> mankind's grief become God's
> and joyfulness come to man,
> when usually each one
> is estranged from the other. (79)

The problem for human beings, for whom St. John speaks in his poems, is that their very means of knowing God can keep them separate from God. For a Christian like St. John of the Cross, the body's senses may exalt him, but they also make him sin, which leads to death:

> Take me away from this dying,
> my God, and give me back to life:
> do not hold me down like this,
> bound up here so tightly. (33)

And yet if the body were actually an incarnation of God, it would not sin or die. Here is the crux of Christian anxiety in the Renaissance and after. If the body is our only way of knowing

God, and if the soul can express itself only in physical terms, how can a transcendent divinity exist? Recognizing this anxiety, St. John of the Cross resorts to his ultimate paradox. In "There Is No Kind of Beauty," he rejects the testimony of the senses, yet rests his paradox on a sensual image:

> Tell me: from such a lover
> would you receive any pain?
> Of all things in creation,
> only he has no flavor.
> Simple, shapeless and lacking
> all substance and location,
> reveling, there in that something
> that fortune puts into our hands. (57)

A negative definition of the senses still requires an experience of them. Ontologically, we cannot think beyond the body. Christianity's ingenious way of accommodating this limitation is the incarnation, God in the human body of Christ. Nevertheless, what we hear in St. John of the Cross, for all his piety, is a restless pursuit—pursuit itself is one of his metaphors—born of a new uncertainty.

Neither Ken Krabbenhoft nor John Frederick Nims gives us ideal translations of these wonderful poems. As a translator, Nims tends to heat up Michelangelo's poetry, making it more inventive and slangier than it appears in Italian, closer respectively to the poetry of Gerard Manley Hopkins and Nims himself. He does, however, provide background for the poems, notes on their date of publication, and an explanation of his aims as a translator. Krabbenhoft, on the other hand, cools down St. John of the Cross's poetry, mostly forgoing its rhyming and metrical patterns, elements that surely must contribute to the poetry's excitement in Spanish. He produces a serene, detached translator's free verse à la W. S. Merwin. Anyone who wants to get a truer flavor of St. John of the Cross in English should find Willis Barnstone's translation, published thirty years ago, which does attempt to reproduce the Spanish verse forms. Barnstone also provides an extensive background for the poetry, which is more helpful than Krabbenhoft's half-page preface.

In any event, it is good to be reminded of these contrasting but complementary poets of Catholic Europe during the Renaissance. Their poetry reflects a dilemma of faith that persists to this day. If the kingdom of God is, indeed, within us, what then is without, outside, and beyond us?

Where Poems Take Place

In his book *Landscape into Art,* Kenneth Clark makes this profound and simple observation:

> Facts become art through love, which unifies them and lifts them to a higher plane of reality; and in landscape, this all embracing love is expressed through light.

I want to talk about how this happens, as I think it does happen, in the kind of poem that takes a particular landscape for its setting. It may do so for dramatic effect, but often it does so because the poet recognizes the landscape as typical of a region or place that he or she loves. If the poet were a landscape painter, then, as Clark states, that love would be expressed through light. Although light does play a role directly or indirectly in each of the six poems I am going to talk about, I would rather use another, analogous term. I want a more inclusive term than *imagery, figure of speech, rhythm,* or even *diction,* yet one as specific as *light.* I am going to borrow the term *phrasing* from music and suggest that in these poems where landscape plays such an important part, the poet's love for the facts of the landscape is expressed through phrasing. Sometimes it is made up of a passage or a line or part of a line. Sometimes it is abstract or imagistic or metaphorical. Sometimes it is musical or has a distinct rhythm. Sometimes it is distinctly flat. Whatever the rhetorical form, the phrasing is always memorable and occurs in response to the landscape and the things that are part of it, and sometimes the people, too.

Robinson Jeffers loved the landscape of the central and

From *The Tennessee Quarterly* (spring 1994).

northern California coast and especially Carmel Bay, where out of ocean boulders he built a house and a tower for himself, his wife, and his two sons. His poem "Tor House" imagines the place long after his work is in ruins or has vanished altogether:

> If you should look for this place after a handful of lifetimes:
> Perhaps of my planted forest a few
> May stand yet, dark-leaved Australians or the coast cypress, haggard
> With storm-drift; but fire and the axe are devils.
> Look for foundations of sea-worn granite, my fingers had the art
> To make stone love stone, you will find some remnant.
> But if you should look in your idleness after ten thousand years:
> It is the granite knoll on the granite
> And lava tongue in the midst of the bay, by the mouth of the Carmel
> River-valley, these four will remain
> In the change of names. You will know it by the wild sea-fragrance of wind
> Though the ocean may have climbed or retired a little;
> You will know it by the valley inland that our sun and our moon were born from
> Before the poles changed; and Orion in December
> Evenings was strung in the throat of the valley like a lamp-lighted bridge.
> Come in the morning you will see white gulls
> Weaving a dance over blue water, the wane of the moon
> Their dance-companion, a ghost walking
> By daylight, but wider and whiter than any bird in the world.
> My ghost you needn't look for; it is probably
> Here, but a dark one, deep in the granite, not dancing on wind
> With the mad wings and the day moon.

Those "dark-leaved Australians" in line 3 are eucalyptus trees, originally imported to California as a source of lumber. They turned out not to be any good for that, but excellent as wind-breaks. Jeffers's use of epithets, often made up of compound adjectives or nouns, derives in part from his love for the poetry of Thomas Hardy, who worked inventively with the form. Along with "dark-leaved Australians," Jeffers gives us "coast cypress, haggard / With storm-drift," "sea-worn granite," "wild sea-fragrance of wind," the moon as a "dance-companion," and in the most beautiful image in the poem the constellation Orion as "a lamp-lighted bridge." In these phrases, there are both firmness and compression, as we find in sound masonry, the exact fit of word loving word as stone loves stone. They reflect Jeffers's love for the place.

There is something else in the natural landscape, both of the earth and the sky, that Jeffers loves. That is evidence of stretches of time so great they are nearly unimaginable. Yet he represents them with a canny familiarity in the first line, "If you should look for this place after a handful of lifetimes," and then further on, "But if you should look in your idleness after ten thousand years." He knows that every thirteen thousand years the location of the celestial poles changes 180 degrees. He mentions that the river valley, which he describes as the place where Orion comes up, will lie along a different east-west axis in ten thousand years. He knows that in the amounts of time he foresees, both man and nature will have no doubt destroyed what he has made. The planet's very place in the cosmos will have altered.

We don't hear Jeffers's so-called double pentameter line in this poem. Rhythm is loosely based on iambs and anapests and on enjambment. We can hear the iambic measure in a phrase like, "My ghost you needn't look for," but the full complement of his metrical variations occurs in the last three lines:

> My ghost you needn't look for; it is probably
> Here, but a dark one, deep in the granite, not dancing on
> wind
> With the mad wings and the day moon.

Alliteration helps him fix the stresses, and the last line is a masterful combination of unstressed and stressed syllables. Parallel repetition, or anaphora, is also an essential element of the sort of free verse Jeffers wrote. He repeats the beginning phrases "If you should" and "You will know it" not only for emphasis but to sustain the rhythm.

Though I am moved by the idea of his ghost being lodged deep in the granite, typically refusing to participate in any merriment like dancing, I have my doubts about the last seven lines of the poem. After the dour certainty of geological and cosmic change expressed by the preceding lines, Jeffers's weather forecast with its blue water and white day moon seems too hopeful. Still, we glimpse a sense of belief in these lines and a love for the world that I find best expressed in lines 10 and 11. First, he locates Tor House as precisely as possible for some future idler, pointing out "the granite knoll on the granite / And lava tongue in the midst of the bay, by the mouth of the Carmel / River-valley. . . ." Then, he makes a statement of faith: "these four will remain / In the change of names." To me this is the most moving response he makes to the landscape; it is the phrasing from the poem that clings most strongly to my memory.

Nostalgia and a changed perspective, as when one grows up and moves away from home, can render a known landscape all the more vivid, especially if one understands it at last. Ellen Bryant Voigt's "Landscape, Dense with Trees" looks back at a landscape with both wisdom and longing:

When you move away, you see how much depends
on the pace of the days—how much
depended on the haze we waded through
each summer, visible heat, wavy and discursive
as the lazy track of the snake in the dusty road;
and on the habit in town of porches thatched in vines;
and in the country long dense promenades, the way
we sacrificed the yards to shade.
It was partly the heat that made my father
plant so many trees—two maples marking the site
for the house, two elms on either side when it was done;
mimosa by the fence, and as it failed, fast-growing chestnuts,
loblolly pines; and dogwood, redbud, ornamental crab.
On the farm, everything else he grew
something could eat, but this
would be a permanent mark of his industry,

a glade established in the open field. Or so it seemed.
Looking back at the empty house from across the hill,
I see how well the house is camouflaged, see how
that porous fence of saplings, their later
scrim of foliage, thickened around it,
and still he chinked and mortared, planting more.
Last summer, although he'd lost all tolerance for heat,
he backed the truck in at the family grave
and stood in the truckbed all afternoon, pruning
the landmark oak, repairing recent damage by a wind;
then he came home and hung a swing
in one of the horse-chestnuts for my visit.
The heat was a hand at his throat,
a fist to his weak heart. But it made a triumph
of the cooler air inside, in the bedroom,
in the maple bedstead where he slept,
in the brick house nearly swamped by leaves.

If we do not know that Voigt grew up in Virginia, there is
enough here to know the general whereabouts. If not the heat,
then the porches and promenades; if not them, then the snake
track in the road; and if not that, then surely the dogwoods and
redbuds tell us this is the rural South, a territory so fertile it can
be made into poetry on its own terms. Thus the "visible heat" is
"wavy and discursive / as the lazy track of the snake in the dusty
road." That rhyming of images, that symmetry, is painterly in it-
self. There is a similar sort of rhyming between the porous fence
of saplings that her father chinked and mortared and the house
it surrounds. The house itself is brick, and it is suggested that if
he didn't build it himself, he did choose the site and mark it
with two maples. His industry gives meaning—artistry—to so
much, it appears that the poet's job is to record his created land-
scape as faithfully as possible. The poet's job is to make phrases
that will simply reflect the love with which the father planted his
trees:

two maples marking the site
for the house, two elms on either side when it was done;
mimosa by the fence, and as it failed, fast-growing chestnuts,
loblolly pines; and dogwood, redbud, ornamental crab.

And without too much obvious artifice, I might add. Just as the house is hidden in that "glade established in the open field," so the conversational meter of Frostian blank verse is hidden in the poem's free verse lineation. Only one line really announces itself as iambic pentameter:

> and still he chinked and mortared, planting more.

Otherwise, the meter is hidden by enjambment, as in:

> the way
> we sacrificed the yards to shade.

Or by added syllables and feet, as in:

> a glade established in the open field. Or so it seemed.

Or by stretched anapestic lines, as in:

> as the lazy track of the snake in the dusty road.

Finally, parallel repetition closes the poem with its own insistent, triumphant, yet improvisatory music:

> in the bedroom,
> in the maple bedstead where he slept,
> in the brick house nearly swamped with leaves.

Hidden at the heart of his work is the father dying of heat exhaustion and the labors of love. All the poet has to do is record his acts, how, for example, he "hung a swing / in one of the horse-chestnuts" for her visit. But in order to see them so clearly, she has to understand them, too. That can take years and even require an irrevocable loss. This poem is full of that understanding. The sense of loss and the mood of elegy are established halfway through the poem with the lines that convey the poet's moment of insight:

> Looking back at the empty house from across the hill,
> I see how well the house is camouflaged. . . .

Love both hid the house and was hidden inside of it, but thanks to the poet's careful rendering of this landscape, we see it now.

Because of the tradition of landscape painting, we tend to think of *landscape* as referring to settings outside the city or the suburbs. Lynda Hull's "Shore Leave" crosses from the urban to the marginally pastoral, as it does also from exterior landscapes to interior ones:

She wears the sailor suit—a blouse with anchors,
skirt puffed in stiff tiers above her thin
knees, those spit-shined party shoes. Behind her
a Cadillac's fabulous fins gleam and reflected
in the showroom window, her father's a mirage.
The camera blocks his face as he frames
a shot that freezes her serious grin,
the splendid awkwardness of almost adolescence.
He's all charm with the car dealer and fast-talks
them a test-drive in a convertible like the one
on display, a two-tone Coupe de Ville. But once
around the corner he lowers the top and soon
they're fishtailing down dump-truck paths,
the Jersey Meadows smoldering with trash fires.
He's shouting *Maybelline, why can't you be true,*
and seagulls lift in a tattered curtain across
Manhattan's hazy skyline. Dust-yellow clouds
behind him, he's handsome as a matinee idol,
wavy hair blown straight by sheer velocity.
Tall marsh weeds bend, radiant as her heart's
relentless tide. They rip past gaping Frigidaires,
rusted hulks of cranes abandoned to the weather.
Her father teases her she's getting so pretty
he'll have to jump ship sometime and take her
on a real whirl, maybe paint the whole town red.
For her *merchant marine* conjures names like
condiments—Malabar, Marseilles—places where
the laws of gravity don't hold. She can't believe
her father's breakneck luck will ever run out.
He accelerates and spins out as if the next thrill
will break through to some more durable joy.
So she stands, hands atop the windshield and shouts
the chorus with him, and later when they drop the car
he takes her to a cocktail bar and plays Chuck Berry

on the jukebox. She perches on a barstool and twirls
her Shirley Temple's paper umbrella, watches
the slick vinyl disks stack up, rhythms collecting,
breaking like surf as her father asks the barmaid
to dance with him through "Blue Moon," then foamy
glass after glass of beer. The barmaid's sinuous
in red taffeta, a rhinestone choker around
her throat. Her father's forgotten her and dances
a slow, slow tango in the empty bar and the dark
comes on like the tiny black rose on the barmaid's
shoulder rippling under her father's hand.
The girl thinks someday she'll cover her skin
with roses, then spins, dizzy on the barstool.
She doesn't hear the woman call her foolish
mortal father a two-bit trick because she's whirling
until the room's a band of light continuous
with the light the city's glittering showrooms throw
all night long over the sleek, impossible cars.

Nothing here is going to last—not the ride, not the junk in
the Jersey Meadows, which are themselves meadows in name
only, at least the part Hull describes, not her father's flirtation
with the barmaid who calls him "a two-bit trick," and not her visit
with her father, who is on shore leave that will end soon. Out of
these details and the landscape they form and are part of comes
the idea of lasting happiness, expressed in the poem's most
memorable phrase: "as if the next thrill / will break through to
some more durable joy." These joys will not last, as I said, but
what durability they do have exists in the Cadillac showroom win-
dow, the dump-truck paths and "the Jersey Meadows smoldering
with trash fires," the "gaping Frigidaires, / rusted hulks of cranes
abandoned to the weather," that "tattered curtain" of seagulls
across the New York City skyline, and the "foolish / mortal" fa-
ther himself. That is, in the poem's phrasing.

The poem ends by contrasting dark and light. First, the dark
"comes on like the tiny black rose on the barmaid's / shoulder
rippling under her father's hand." And then the girl, whirling
on her barstool, is able to make the bar a "band of light con-
tinuous / with the light the city's glittering showrooms throw /
all night long over the sleek, impossible cars." This is both

painterly and cinematic. A cinematic blending of images predominates in the poem and is first represented by the father's image, "a mirage," reflected in the showroom window as he takes his daughter's picture.

The images have a high gloss blurred by speed, the poem's headlong rhythm. It is the rhythm of the poem that is largely responsible for its glamour and grandeur, even in the tawdriest parts of these landscapes, as the poem memorializes a day. A kind of blank verse, measured by ear and eye, is at work here, running on with enjambments too quickly for us to stop and measure a line. As with Voigt's poem, we can see that iambic pentameter is the model. The very first line announces it: "She wears the sailor suit—a blouse with anchors." We hurry on as if by holding as much as possible, putting as much as possible in the frame or the landscape, the poet could either stop time or make it continuous with the present. There is an excessive fullness to many of the phrases. The father's tango is not just slow but "slow, slow"; the cars are not only "sleek" but "impossible"; and the father, though he has amply demonstrated his character, is both "foolish" and "mortal." The phrasing bears a heavy freight of love to offset the flimsiness of what is loved.

I hope we can hear the pastoral history with all its idealized landscapes in the phrase "Jersey Meadows," just as the poet claims to have heard the exotic and faraway in "Malabar, Marseilles." And I don't want to forget that here the loved landscape, as in Voigt's poem, owes much of its value to the presence of the father and the poet's love for him. Where Voigt's poem bestows understanding on the landscape her father created, Hull's bestows worth and durability on the transient and worthless.

If Kenneth Clark's statement about the role of light in landscape painting can apply to any of these poems, it certainly applies to Garrett Hongo's "Yellow Light":

> One arm hooked around the frayed strap
> of a tar-black patent-leather purse,
> the other cradling something for dinner:
> fresh bunches of spinach from a J-Town *yaoya*,
> sides of split Spanish mackerel from Alviso's,

maybe a loaf of Langendorf; she steps
off the hissing bus at Olympic and Fig,
begins the three-block climb up the hill,
passing gangs of schoolboys playing war,
Japs against Japs, Chicanas chalking sidewalks
with the holy double-yoked crosses of hopscotch,
and the Korean grocer's wife out for a stroll
around this neighborhood of Hawaiian apartments
just starting to steam with cooking
and the anger of young couples coming home
from work, yelling at kids, flicking on
TV sets for the Wednesday night fights.

If it were May, hydrangeas and jacaranda
flowers in the streetside trees would be
blooming through the smog of late spring.
Wisteria in Masuda's front yard would be
shaking out the long tresses of its purple hair.
Maybe mosquitoes, moths, a few orange butterflies
settling on the lattice of monkey flowers
tangled in chain-link fences by the trash.

But this is October, and Los Angeles
seethes like a billboard under twilight.

From used-car lots and the movie houses uptown,
long silver sticks of light probe the sky.
From the Miracle Mile, whole freeways away,
a brilliant fluorescence breaks out
and makes war with the dim squares
of yellow kitchen light winking on
in all the side streets of the Barrio.

She climbs up the two flights of flagstone
stairs to 201-B, the spikes of her high heels
clicking like kitchen knives on a cutting board,
props the groceries against the door,
fishes through memo pads, a compact,
empty packs of chewing gum, and finds her keys.

The moon then, cruising from behind
a screen of eucalyptus across the street,
covers everything, everything in sight,
in a heavy light like yellow onions.

This is very much a peopled landscape, and its population, diversely Asian and Hispanic, is typical of the part of Los Angeles around the intersection of Olympic Boulevard and Figueroa Street (the "Fig" of line 7). The poet loves these people and this place, along with the names of local stores and products (Alviso's, Langendorf bread, Japantown with its green grocers or *yaoya*'s), the weather (smog), and the architecture (the apartments in the so-called Hawaiian style, probably with pastel stucco walls and some scruffy subtropical landscaping). Tension exists right on the surface of this urban pastoral. It is stated frankly at the ends of stanzas 1 and 2, in the couplet of stanza 3, in the sources of light making war in the fourth stanza, and in the sound of the spiked high heels in stanza 5. The moon cruises in, like a cop car or a driver looking for action, and throws an ambiguous light, suggesting both the spice of good cooking with its healing powers and the onion skins that are peeled off to reveal the raw, tear-inducing flesh beneath them. Hinted at, too, in the final stanza are the redolent fragrance of eucalyptus and the protective nature of the trees. Much of the poem is flatly stated, but it is complexly satisfying.

Behind the poem is Whitman, the Great Cataloguer of Democracy. The rhythm is his parallel repetition, in the food in the woman's arms, the people she passes in her neighborhood, the list of spring flowers, the sources of light elsewhere in the city, the action of the woman looking for her door keys, and the pay-off—the repetition of "everything, everything in sight." But another tradition feeds the poem, too, and that is the haiku. This is a hell of a long haiku, but the insight inherent in the natural detail, in all of these natural details, is conveyed as it would be in a haiku. Look at the couplet. After the lyrical passage about spring in downtown L.A., we are given a poem about fall there:

> But this is October, and Los Angeles
> seethes like a billboard under twilight.

How do I translate that? The season is dry, hot, brilliant. In the transition of twilight, the city is about to turn from one side of itself to another, like a billboard just before or after its floodlights come on. It is hard to paraphrase a haiku.

A couple of phrases that grow out of this landscape and show the poet's feeling for it—a feeling that almost transcends love—are "the smog of late spring," a phrase that is, unfortunately, perfectly accurate, and the description of the Miracle Mile, the business district of Wilshire Boulevard, as being "whole freeways away." The latter phrase is exactly on target socially and economically. The worlds of Los Angeles are separated by such distances and barriers, barriers that masquerade as access. The riots in April 1992 demonstrated how these barriers work. And the entire poem takes on a new and painful meaning when we realize that the neighborhood depicted was part of the rioting. The violence Hongo locates in this urban pastoral looks prophetic now.

Poems about landscape tend to ground us. They have a gravity that reminds us that the earth is organized into the world. I want to turn to another poem of the landscape now, but one quite different from the previous ones I have discussed. It is a poem that contrasts the earthly perspective with the desire to be free of it: Robert McDowell's "Test Pilot."

I came here from a Kansas farm

                                   but now I can't feel it.

The whole world is mosaic,
And God a piece of the iris breaking off.
The sun makes flares

                         out of tin roofs
                         out of wings.

The cockpit is a bell.
I throw back the deadbolt in my head;
I throw it back and sing.

I am so loud two horseshoe players stop.
They know they are like grass the mower bites.

Voices on the radio quarrel like birds
Over the carcass of a silo.

They want me back.
They are full of scratch

                                                            but now I can't hear them.

I am so loud   so loud

Look up!

I am like grass.

First, I want to dispel any notion that this poem shares more than a passing sentiment with the corny "High Flight," which begins, "Oh, I have slipped the surly bonds of earth." The difference in the two is specificity—phrasing again. This poem makes the landscape look inward at the intelligence that invests it with meaning. We have been dealing with this figure all along. "Test Pilot" introduces us to it—the light of the mind, here regarding itself. The view is aerial and surreal:

> The whole world is mosaic,
> And God a piece of the iris breaking off.
> The sun makes flares
>
>   out of tin roofs
>   out of wings

Of all the poems examined here this one relies on more than the audible measure of the line to establish its rhythm. The page is used and suggests that on the page the text of the poem is a kind of landscape, that is, if its visual element is exploited. What also interests me is the structure of this poem. It seems to have its roots in the statement and variation form of Biblical poetry; again there is a rhythm based on parallelism. I hear the echo of Biblical language, too, in the reverberations of the final lines, specifically, Isaiah 40:6:

> The voice said, cry. And he said, what shall I cry? All flesh is grass, and all its goodliness is like the flower of the field.

Embedded, like a root or an afterimage, in the ethereal fantasy of this speaker's vision is earthly mortality. Not only are the horseshoe players, weighed down with their game pieces, like grass, but so is the celestial speaker. When he says, "I am like grass," the phrase echoes Isaiah, but it does not share the prophet's stoic resignation. It's turned on, an epiphany of mortality, and expresses the speaker's excitement to locate himself in a new scheme of things, far from home, but still attached to the earth.

I suppose what I admire in all of these poems is that they have a smell of earth about them, even at their most far out, a feeling for the soil of a specific place and for the world's impermanence. Each of them shows us that the poet has looked with love at a landscape and transformed it into art.

A landscape represents an ordering of the eye, even when the depiction is of the wildest disorder, and in that way might be what Frost said a poem was—a momentary stay against confusion. Each of the poems I have talked about so far has told us where to look—for the remains of a dwelling, for a house swamped by leaves, for the illusion of joy, for the keys to a place, for the intelligence that makes the poem. Robert Frost's "Directive" also acknowledges that when we read a poem, we look where the poet tells us to, often at a place or landscape he loves:

> Back out of all this now too much for us,
> Back in a time made simple by the loss
> Of detail, burned, dissolved, and broken off
> Like graveyard marble sculpture in the weather,
> There is a house that is no more a house
> Upon a farm that is no more a farm
> And in a town that is no more a town.
> The road there, if you'll let a guide direct you
> Who only has at heart your getting lost
> May seem as if it should have been a quarry—
> Great monolithic knees the former town
> Long since gave up pretense of keeping covered.
> And there's a story in a book about it:
> Besides the wear of iron wagon wheels
> The ledges show lines ruled southeast-northwest,
> The chisel work of an enormous Glacier
> That braced his feet against the Arctic Pole.
> You must not mind a certain coolness from him
> Still said to haunt this side of Panther Mountain.
> Nor need you mind the serial ordeal
> Of being watched from forty cellar holes
> As if by eye pairs out of forty firkins.
> As for the woods' excitement over you

That sends light rustle rushes to their leaves,
Charge that to upstart inexperience.
Where were they all not twenty years ago?
They think too much of having shaded out
A few old pecker-fretted apple trees.
Make yourself up a cheering song of how
Someone's road home from work this once was,
Who may be just ahead of you on foot
Or creaking with a buggy load of grain.
The height of the adventure is the height
Of country where two village cultures faded
Into each other. Both of them are lost.
And if you're lost enough to find yourself
By now pull in your ladder road behind you
And put a sign up CLOSED to all but me.
Then make yourself at home. The only field
Now left's no bigger than a harness gall.
First there's the children's house of make-believe,
Some shattered dishes underneath a pine,
The playthings in the playhouse of the children.
Weep for what little things could make them glad.
Then for the house that is no more a house,
But only a belilaced cellar hole,
Now slowly closing like a dent in dough.
This was no playhouse but a house in earnest.
Your destination and your destiny's
A brook that was the water of the house,
Cold as a spring as yet so near its source
Too lofty and original to rage.
(We know the valley streams that when aroused
Will leave their tatters hung on barb and thorn.)
I have kept hidden in the instep arch
Of an old cedar at the waterside
A broken drinking goblet like the Grail
Under a spell so the wrong ones can't find it,
So can't get saved, as Saint Mark says they mustn't.
(I stole the goblet from the children's playhouse.)
Here are your waters and your watering place.
Drink and be whole again beyond confusion.

The sly paradox of Frost's directions, what he would call his
mischief or fooling, is that often when he points one way, he

looks another. If there is a guiding figure of speech in "Directive," it is paradox. It affects Frost's personal brands of irony, whimsy, allusion, his way with a country simile, all his phrasing, everything that has to do with this landscape. Although he takes great care in creating this landscape, his is the poem in which we see most clearly that the landscape *is* created, and in this case, out of words. A composite landscape of his other poems, it is like dough in his hands. Nevertheless, we can imagine the place he imagines as existing in the mountains shared by Vermont and New Hampshire.

The very first line, probably the poem's best line, takes us away from Wordsworth's "The world is too much with us, late and soon / Getting and spending we lay waste our powers," and takes us toward true impoverishment, not just a Romantic nostalgia for ancient belief, as in Wordsworth's sonnet. But does Frost lead us back to a living present before this time when the past is memorialized by graves? Paradox may be the presiding mode of the poem (no wonder the New Critics loved Frost), but Frost's paradoxes are more slippery than we might expect and hint subtly that the poem's realities are creations of language. As much attention as he will pay to detail, he is leading us to "a time made simple / By the loss of detail." Or so he says. Yet surely the time-lapse photographic image of the graveyard goes forward. The phrase "burned, dissolved, and broken off / Like graveyard marble sculpture in the weather" suggests some future ruin. And the house, farm, and town that we will be shown are no more what they were. And yet, what they are are the paradoxical phrases that represent them:

> a house that is no more a house
> Upon a farm that is no more a farm
> And in a town that is no more a town.

That is where we are going—a place in the poet's imagination, a landscape made of words.

Like Jeffers, Frost loves the history embedded in stretches of geological time. These are spans so great, they offer themselves to play. (Jeffers even indulges in it, if you think about his ghost hidden in the granite in "Tor House.") The town no longer primly covers the great stone knees along the road. The ledges show not only human presence, but the inhuman artistry—the chisel work—of a glacier that may still be around. The glacier's coolness will be echoed in the brook's coldness. His aloofness will return in the brook's loftiness and originality. Like the frost that shows its crystal teeth in the water of "Two Tramps in Mudtime," Frost's own face in miragelike self-portraits looks back at us from this landscape.

A more compressed sense of elapsed time follows with the eyes in the cellar holes (all the houses are no more, like the one we are going to), and like the glacier, the woods, too, are alive, personified, excited with their own fairly recent flourishing. Frost is leading us into more densely wooded, spookier territory. He wants us to be apprehensive (even if we don't feel that way). In the shade of the new trees are older ones, old apple trees, punctured by woodpeckers, but also bearing the poet's signature. Plant apple trees in an American poem, and people are going to think of Robert Frost. They're his property, part of his landscape. These woods, like this side of Panther Mountain, are haunted.

The landscape is mountainous; we have been climbing. The word *height* can be taken two ways. It is figurative. Our adventure's climax lies ahead. And it is literal, if it means some ridge or peak. Though perhaps this is figurative, too, if Frost has in mind a time when village or country culture reached its apex before it disappeared. Two village cultures. As I have suggested before, they may have met at the border of Vermont and New Hampshire.

Frost, who is always playing for mortal stakes, turns the road into a rope ladder the reader can pull in. The CLOSED sign is another whimsical touch, but the disturbing thing about it is the suggestion that our guide is behind us, having sent us on with directions, assuming that once we'd lost ourselves he could join us. There is a touch of the Zen master or spiritual leader in this attitude. We have gone on ahead, but he's already been there before us and may or may not be with us in spirit.

We can make ourselves at home, but we can't make ourselves *a* home. Irony refreshes this cliché. To say, "the only field / Now left's no bigger than a harness gall" is not only to employ a form of country simile, but to do so for what is implied by "harness gall." The size may be exaggerated in its smallness, although the trees have hemmed in everything. The point is that the field is painfully small. That is a phrase that gives us a landscape in plain English the landscape itself can understand.

We have to imagine the rest based on ruins: shattered dishes for a playhouse, a cellar hole for a house. There's a bit of poetry in the word *belilaced,* but there is also the stuff of genius in describing the hole as "slowly closing like a dent in dough." Frost plays as he details the destruction. "Playthings" are played off "playhouse," "playhouse" is played off "house in earnest." We are told to weep, as we are told earlier to sing. I'm not sure we can right away. Later, maybe, as the poem comes back to haunt us.

We are now in the world of the Grail legend, a totally mythical one, with allusions to one of the great quest stories and to the Gospel of St. Mark. The following passage from St. Mark, 4:10–11, was a favorite of Frost's. It comes after Jesus has told the parable of the sower:

> And when he was alone, those who were about him with the twelve asked him concerning parables. And he said to them, "To you has been given the secret of the kingdom of God, but for those outside everything is in parables; so that they may indeed hear but not understand; lest they should turn again, and be forgiven."

Ironically, after flattering his listeners' intelligence, Jesus must still explain to them the parable of the sower. We get no such explanation from Frost. In that hidden drinking goblet I hear another allusion to a poet, like Wordsworth, that Frost both admired and either corrected or adapted. Thomas Hardy's "Under the Waterfall" includes a similar drinking goblet, this one dropped into a small cascade and wedged out of reach. The speaker of Hardy's poem says that whenever she dips her arm in a basin of water, she recalls fishing for the dropped drinking glass. Hardy's is a love poem. Frost assures us that his goblet is stolen from the children's playhouse. It is "a broken drinking goblet like the Grail." Was the Grail broken? Well, here it is. He has hidden it under the instep arch of an old cedar, which is endowed like the glacier and the woods with humanity by that bit of personification. This poem gives us a lesson in how the pathetic fallacy can work for a poet.

Our destination and our destiny have been to pass through and end up at a place, a landscape, created before our eyes. If we drink from the waters we are offered, our confusion will be dispelled by a wellspring of genius. Our own sense of fragmentation, mirrored in the ruins the poem lingers over, will be made whole.

Out of words; out of literature, like the Bible, the Grail legend, the poetry of Wordsworth and Hardy, the poetry of Frost himself; out of country speech and country things that speech preserves, Frost makes this whole—the poem.

I am thinking now of two lines from other poems by Frost that have something to do with where I have ended up in this discussion of landscape in poetry, which is also a discussion of poetry's power to transform the world. One line is from the long narrative poem "The Mountain." It is a line of dialogue tossed off by a local character who has been toying with an outsider, also on a matter of directions. He says, "But all the fun's in how you say a thing." The other line comes from the beautiful lyric "Mowing": "The fact is the sweetest dream that labor knows." Something about poetry that has always impressed and challenged and intimidated me is that you have to make up your own raw material. Words may be your facts, but they have themselves to be made into facts, and those facts, as Kenneth Clark says, become art through love. That love may be complex, but part of its essence and its power to transform must be the love of making art, which is both a labor of love and, as Frost suggests in "The Mountain," a kind of play, too. After all, in poetry, "all the fun's in how you say a thing."

I have ended far from where I began. I started by talking about where poems take place and moved from earthly landscapes to the poet's imagination. I guess in more general terms I am talking not just about landscape but about any poem's subject and not only about phrasing but about all the words in a poem. I believe that poetry is a representational art. None of the poems I have discussed would convince us of its location in place, its depiction of a landscape, if there was not also a sense that the words were not only creating but recreating something. That something is the subject that moves the poet. Love of that subject—a landscape, a face—is not enough, of course. A poet has to love the labor it requires to transform it into art.

In *Landscape into Art*, Kenneth Clark locates the beginning of modern landscape painting in the background of a Dutch manuscript, the *Hours of Turin*, by Hubert van Eyck. In one panel, William of Bavaria, posed in the chivalric manner, lands on a beach. But behind him the seashore is rendered, as Clark says, "completely outside the fifteenth-century range of responsiveness." Light sparkles on little waves. In contrast to the conventional foreground, you can tell what the artist really cared about.

A Shared Humanity

These are my customs and establishments.
It would be much more serious to refuse.
—Philip Larkin,
"The Importance of Elsewhere"

A man who ought to know me
wrote in a review
my emotional life was meagre.
—Donald Davie, "July, 1964"

In his collection of lectures, *Czeslaw Milosz and the Insufficiency of Lyric,* Donald Davie argues that, because of twentieth-century history, the lyric poet has lost the privilege of being responsible only to himself and his emotions. Therefore, he must find a way to speak for more than himself. The late-twentieth-century search for a more representative self is not peculiar to our era. Keats sought it in his attempts at empathy, in the very negative capability now associated with the self-involved lyric and against which Davie reacts. Davie himself has sought in his poems a larger expression, while at the same time acknowledging the limits of the lyric which make such an expression impossible. "In the Stopping Train," one of Davie's finest poems, is an attempt to understand the insufficiency of lyric by subjecting the poet himself to nearly merciless critical examination.

It is helpful to compare Davie's poem, from his 1977 volume of the same name, with the title poem of Philip Larkin's 1964 collection, *The Whitsun Weddings.* "In the Stopping Train" seems, in part, a response to "The Whitsun Weddings," not merely because

From *On Modern Poetry,* a festschrift for Donald Davie, edited by Laurence Lerner and Vereen Bell (Nashville: Vanderbilt University Press, 1988).

both record journeys on stopping or local trains, but because the former presents a totally different role for the poet than the latter. The irony is that Larkin, in his poem, is not nearly as wrapped up in himself as Davie is. Yet Larkin's detachment from his subject has been cause for serious criticism, and quite rightly.

First of all, justifying his own ways to his fellow men has never been the problem for Larkin that it is for Davie, except as Larkin has been too much like other people, letting "the toad work squat" on his life, for example, or not enough like them, as in "Annus Mirabilis," where he admits to being a very late bloomer. Larkin is at his best when posing as the curious observer or when absent altogether. His self-effacement has been called smugness, though it might be seen as modesty. Davie's self-examination is not its opposite exactly, but more a search for humility, for atonement. But Davie is a Christian poet, and Larkin is not.

Existential anxiety is not present in "The Whitsun Weddings." Once Larkin boards his train on a hot Saturday afternoon at Whitsuntide, he feels "all sense / Of being in a hurry gone." The windows are down, the cushions are hot, but he pretty much has the car to himself, and after observing the urban landscape giving way to countryside as the train makes its way from Hull to London, he begins to read. The landscape is important to Larkin, especially as it retains its rural features and as they are lost or marred. Despite the poem's fame, the second stanza is worth quoting entirely:

> All afternoon, through the tall heat that slept
>   For miles inland,
> A slow and stopping curve southwards we kept.
> Wide farms went by, short-shadowed cattle, and
> Canals with floatings of industrial froth;
> A hothouse flashed uniquely: hedges dipped
> And rose: and now and then a smell of grass
> Displaced the reek of buttoned carriage-cloth
> Until the next town, new and nondescript,
> Approached with acres of dismantled cars.

All of Larkin's strengths are present here, including his love of and doubts about pastoral England; his eye for the telling image—those cattle, that hothouse, those canals; his extraordinary gift for the simple yet perfect imagistic phrase—"the tall heat"; and even his way of pointing to a poem's central intelligence—the annoyed reference to "the reek of buttoned carriage-cloth." Yet it is the little drama of the poem, beginning in the third stanza and continuing through the next six until the end, that requires an assessment of Larkin's particular, even peculiar temperament as a lyric poet. It requires one because, in this poem at least, none is offered by the poet himself.

Both American and British critics have noted Larkin's superior air in this poem. Blake Morrison in his book *The Movement* says that Larkin "seems to patronize as well as to pity" the working-class wedding parties he observes at each train depot. Merle Brown in an essay on Larkin's audience published in the *Iowa Review* in 1977 is downright censorious, but puts his finger on the problem of how much the lyric poet can represent himself and others. Brown writes:

> In "The Whitsun Weddings" . . . Larkin takes on the sovereign privileges of . . . invisible, unnameable observing even though he also presents himself as a visible, existent entity. He should have recognized that such a hybrid is inadmissible in poetry the likes of his. By bringing the act of attending into the scene, he has unknowingly committed an obscenity, in the sense that he has brought on stage what by its nature must occur offstage.

Strong stuff. But what Larkin has done in this poem is no more than what Tolstoy does in *War and Peace,* except that it violates our expectations of the first-person point of view, especially in a poem where we implicitly take that point of view to be the poet's own.

Larkin presumes to understand what is going on in the minds and hearts of the people he sees. Once he realizes the noise at each stop is not merely workers on the platforms but truly an event—the last weddings of the Whitsun week, portions of festivals that have marked the week for centuries—he is interested: "Struck, I leant / More promptly out next time, more curiously, / And saw it all again in different terms." Granted, the catalogue of Larkinesque caricatures that follows is smugly satirical. On the platforms waving goodbye to the newlyweds are fathers with "seamy foreheads," "mothers loud and fat," "an uncle shouting smut," and girls in their "parodies of fashion," including "jewellery-substitutes." Yet Larkin's eye is typically English, picking out as it does the limited expectations, the cheapness at the end of empire. What he sees has been a theme of British literature at least since World War II. But Larkin penetrates the phenomenon more deeply here, understanding it even as he seems to push it away, and to do this he assumes an omniscience based on shared experience. He observes that this event is witnessed in different ways, by children as "dull," by fathers as "success . . . huge and wholly farcical," by the women as a "secret like a happy funeral," and by the girls themselves as "a religious wounding": "Free at last, / And loaded with the sum of all they saw, / We hurried towards London. . . ."

Critics of this poem point out that Larkin either fails or refuses to see his place among the dozen marriages that have "got underway" on the train with him, and that he presumes even further to speak for the newlyweds, when he notes, "none / Thought of the others they would never meet / Or how their lives would all contain this hour." Only he sees this coming together, "this frail / Travelling coincidence," when in fact he is the odd man out. Although we might express irritation with him, to censor him is to deny the emotional accuracy of the poem. His removal from the others, his difference from them, may have resulted in complacent self-regard, but it is not alienation. It does allow him to see the event whole, and his personal affection for it is related to his love for England itself. When he recognizes what is going on, his response is "Yes." Larkin affirms the persistence of Whitsun festivities. He also affirms the weddings themselves with the blessing that ends the poem, when he imagines that, after the train stops, what it holds will continue on "like an arrow-shower / Sent out of sight, somewhere becoming rain." Finally, however we may object to the condescending tone of this; the emotion is not one that any of the other passengers would have had; rather, it is one felt for them.

"In the Stopping Train" may be the poem Larkin's critics are looking for in "The Whitsun Weddings." Davie's train passenger would enjoy Larkin's serene outward look, too, if he believed it would do any good. But Davie's rage is inward and is aimed precisely at what divides him from others, including himself. The rhythm of "The Whitsun Weddings" is unhurried. Its eight ten-line stanzas rhyme ababcdecde; five of the eight dovetail with the stanza following them; all but the second line of each stanza is in iambic pentameter; only that line, in iambic dimeter, registers the jolt of the train's stopping and starting, if it is meant to imitate anything. Davie's poem, in ten unnumbered parts, with stanzas appearing as couplets, tercets, quatrains, does not flow smoothly from strophe to strophe over bright knots of rhyme like Larkin's. Instead, it reflects in its lurching, enjambed, trimeter lines not only the speaker's anguish but the train's frustrating stop and start. Davie's train trip is neither as comfortable nor as magisterial as Larkin's. His poem lacks, too, Larkin's sweeping way with metaphor that allows him to speak of well-wishers left behind on boarding platforms "as if out on the end of an event / Waving goodbye / To something that survived it." But Davie's cramped, self-analytical ride does give us a narrative structure that exists as more than a route to an end. It is the mode by which the commonplace event—taking the train somewhere—is invested with the urgency to have understood oneself before the end of the journey. Davie's poem, then, has the greater symbolic and emotional resonance.

The first part of "In the Stopping Train" gets right to the matter, yet at the same time it begins probing for the heart of the poet's unhappiness:

> I have got into the slow train
> again. I made the mistake
> knowing what I was doing,
> knowing who had to be punished.
>
> I know who has to be punished:
> the man going mad inside me;
> whether I am fleeing
> from him or towards him.

The tone of puritanical self-loathing is quite clear, but is boarding this train "again" a recurrent error or, as he implies, a deliberate punishment? The self divided from the self has to be punished, in part, for his lack of charity:

> He abhors his fellows,
> especially children; let there
> not for pity's sake
> be a crying child in the carriage.
>
> So much for pity's sake.

This is the first of the bitterly humorous remarks made at the speaker's own expense throughout the poem. Is there a crying child on the carriage to whom the "So much for pity's sake" has been directed? Or does the wish defeat any notion of pity, even that suggested by the expression "for pity's sake"? The fascination of this poem is the total lack of objectivity. No flowers will be observed, no architecture or landscapes will be noted simply for pleasure as in the Larkin poem. Instead, language about them will be analyzed:

> Jonquil is a sweet word.
> Is it a flowering bush?
> Let him helplessly wonder
> for hours if perhaps he's seen it.

Davie zeroes in on the culprit—it is the artist, the man going mad inside him with a self-involved passion, who "never needed to see, / not with his art to help him." It is this figure, too, who has hatreds and loves, though false. He is the passionate figure who, for reasons not yet clear aside from his selfishness, must be punished.

Meanwhile, he displays for us his various artistic and intellectual strengths as he tries to understand his situation. The play of language, of tones of voice, and of rhythm predominates in Davie's poem, whereas in Larkin's imagery and metaphor are foremost. The second part of "In the Stopping Train" contains the most moving of Davie's wordplay; it is affecting because it touches on the larger symbolism of this ride:

> A stopping train, I thought,
> was a train that was going to stop.
> Why board it then, in the first place?
>
> Oh no, they explained, it is stopping
> and starting, stopping and starting.

Here, "they" are adults; the exchange recalls their voices. In this section there *is* a child in the carriage after all. Having understood the adult assurances, Davie says, "I saw the logic of that; / grown-ups were good at explaining." But the starting and the stopping of the train does not keep it from getting to the end of the line. As broad as the hint becomes here—"even expresses have to do that"—still, there is a power in this internal dialogue, this analysis of memory. The child Davie is not sure the adults understand his anxiety about riding such a train, and the adults show this by ending the conversation:

> Well, they said, you'll learn
> all about that when you're older.
>
> Of course they learned it first.
> Oh naturally, yes.

Is it mortality, then, that has been the source of the inner man's, the artist's madness? The resentful tone of the last lines is mitigated by one of resignation. This is one of the poem's quietest moments.

Davie shows a distinct temperament in the third part; that is, it is distinct from Larkin's ironic detachment. Regarding the reckless traffic on the highway that runs beside the train, the "passing and re-passing" of cars with "a recklessness like breeding," "he is shrieking silently: 'Rabbits!'" To follow this with the refrain "He abhors his fellows" may be seen as an understatement. Yet the British use of the rabbit, despite its cutesified transformation in *Watership Down,* is instructive. Larkin's "Myxomatosis," ostensibly about the disease spread to control the rabbit population in Britain after World War II, ends with lines that could be meant to indict an aspect of the British character: "You may have thought things would come right again / If you could only keep quite still and wait." And there is in *The Wind and the Willows*, of all places, Kenneth Grahame's characterization of the rabbits who never wish to be involved, whose response is "*Do* something? Us rabbits?" Davie's epithet here may carry these connotations, along with the angry one of the sterile condemning the mindlessly procreative. Yet, this dissonance is resolved:

> Yet even the meagre arts
> of television can
> restore them to him sometimes,
>
> when the man in uniform faces
> the unrelenting camera
> with a bewildered fierceness
> beside the burnt-out Simca.

Confronted by the record of urban, probably terrorist violence, in which "his fellows," individuals like those he has been cursing, have been victimized and the representative of order, "the man in uniform," must make sense for the masses watching, Davie is capable of that which he claims to lack—pity, perhaps even charity.

Lest we be seduced by this harmonic moment, however, the splenetic voice returns in the fourth part, growling, "What's all this about flowers?" He observes that "some people claim to love them." Here the poet is faced with the full power of a word's meaning and the need to justify it to his own intelligence:

> Love *them?* Love flowers? Love,
> love . . . the word is hopeless:
> gratitude, maybe, pity . . .
>
> Pitiful, the flowers.

Again, as with the rueful "So much for pity's sake," the notion of pity being misaligned with its object has wit. But "love" is the most important word in the poem, the word the poem resolves on, its last word, in fact. These flowers are pitiful because they are merely words, or merely a word, and the poet "can name them all, / identify hardly any." The madness, the passion, the spleen here are vented because of an inability or a refusal to apply to reality the names the poet has for it, including "love." Nominalists make for anxious Christians.

The fifth section is interesting because it helps to characterize the speaker, to identify him more closely with Davie. It is subtitled "*Judith Wright, Australian.*" Why would this particular character be thinking about the Australian poet Judith Wright? It would be simple enough to say that, well, Donald Davie is the speaker and he thinks about quite a lot of things to do with English literature, especially contemporary sorts. Has Davie carefully created a fictional self or selves for this poem? We already know the character has a literary bent; here he is giving an opinion that appears first to be gratuitous but, on a closer look, is not. Our speaker is occupying his time with more than internal agony and outward grousing. He is writing or thinking about somebody else:

> Judith Wright, Australian,
> "has become," I said,
>
> "the voice of her unhappy,
> still-to-be-guilty nation."
>
> Wistfully I said it,
> there in the stopping train.

A literary man can be believed to be writing or thinking about a review, for example, as he takes even the most miserable of rides; after all, he has time, and there is leisure to work on a train. Of greater import here, however, is that Davie has recognized that a poet can be the voice of an entire nation. Though guilt is that nation's inheritance, he assigns Wright's voice to it "wistfully," with a melancholy wish. Australia's history has been bound up in England's, though it is no longer. England has had its voices, but the singular spokesman has faded along with empire. For whom today does the contemporary English poet speak? Here he speaks only for himself and his own guilt.

In the sixth part the poem turns and the speaker faces himself:

> The things he has been spared . . .
> "Gross egotist!" Why don't
> his wife, his daughter, shrill
> that in his face?
>
> Love and pity seem
> the likeliest explanations;
> another occurs to him—
> despair too would be quiet.

These lines look back to the rumination of the fifth part and ahead to those parts to come. What he has been spared is any concern for or obligation to anything besides his profession. Here "love and pity" are introduced but this time not as part of a witty self-satire. They are solemn recognitions of his family's indulgence. They are joined by another motive, in a play on Thoreau's famous observation, here personalized and all the more poignant. Our speaker himself is not living a life of quiet desperation, but rather, if his inner turmoil is an indication, of noisy desperation. His self-disgust is partly with the ridiculous figure cut by the ranting inner man. Love, pity, and despair, in the form of those closest to him, regard his anguish sadly and quietly.

The seventh part is the most rhythmically effective of the poem. At this point, rather than apologize, Davie rears up and justifies his professional activities in martial terms:

> Time and again he gave battle,
> furious, mostly effective;
> nobody counts the wear
> and tear of rebuttal.

He has not shrunk from controversy. He has even been proud of the stands he has taken, although there is some question about their lasting importance. Finally, playing on his own favorite metaphor of poetry as sculpture, an art worked in a durable medium, he admits that his own intellect and emotions have been "hardened" by his engagements. One can make a list of the many stands Davie has taken in his career, the areas of intellectual and artistic endeavor he has pronounced for—and against—and recognize this as an honest assessment of the man by the man himself. The phrase "Time and again," which begins each of the section's five quatrains, and the rhymes in each stanza, rare in this poem, give the section its power. Yet the single most powerful stanza in the poem derives its strength from an apparent disruption:

> Time and again, oh time and
> that stopping train!
> Who knows when it comes to a stand,
> and will not start again.

Once more, the emblematic nature of this train is emphasized. The subject and the form could not be more closely welded.

The eighth part brings a change of tone, one that approaches the second stanza of "The Whitsun Weddings." As I have argued, there is a calmness, even a serenity, to Larkin's point of view that allows him to see the big picture, or what he imagines to be the big picture, without coming himself to any sort of intense self-realization. That is not his point, to be sure. Davie, on the other hand, shows us active and painful self-division. As he recognizes this state for what it is, he detaches himself from it, so to speak, and in this section speaks more in Larkin's disinterested tone. The eighth part is also subtitled, in parenthesis, "Son et Lumière." It is as if the window of the stuffy car were opened for a moment:

> I have travelled with him many times
> now. Already we nod,
> we are almost on speaking terms.
>
> Once I thought that he sketched
> an apologetic gesture
> at what we turned away from.

He describes how his traveling companion's glasses caught the light as he turned away, and he comes to the following passage of deft, impressionistic landscape painting:

> I knew they had been ranging,
> paired eyes like mine,
> igniting and occluding
>
> coppice and crisp chateau,
> thatched corner, spray of leaf,
> curved street, a swell of furrows,
>
> where still the irrelevant vales
> were flowering, and the still
> silver rivers slid west.

This is called having your cake and eating it, too. Though the spectacles blind the viewer and though the vales are called "irrelevant," the self-laceration is missing here in words like "crisp," "thatched," "spray," "curved," "swell," "flowering," and "silver." The sounds are gorgeous and forgiving.

Perhaps they hint at a reconciliation not to occur in this poem. An intenser rhythm returns in the ninth part, albeit with a sprightliness that includes a recognition of the landscape's redemptive properties. Here, too, the play of voices is most apparent and effective. If for this character "words alone are certain good," then admitting this leads to a sort of acclamation of what our fellow can do—play with words:

> The dance of words
> is a circling prison, thought
> the passenger staring through
> the hot unmoving pane
> of boredom. It is not
> thank God a dancing pain,
> he thought, though it starts to jig
> now. (The train is moving.) "This,"
> he thought in rising panic
> (Sit down! Sit down!)
> "this much I can command,
> exclude. Dulled words, keep still!
> Be the inadequate, cloddish
> despair of me!" No good:
> they danced, as the smiling land
> fled past the pane, the pun's
> galvanized *tarantelle*.

This may be the most emotionally complicated section of the poem, since the dull words tie him to the earth ("cloddish"), tend to embarrass him as he grows excited about their possibilities ("Sit down! Sit down!"), and bring on a "rising panic" with its connotations of terror and the power of Pan. The "dancing pain" becomes a "jig," and the words, despite Davie's demurral, do dance. The landscape smiles, and the hot boredom of the poet's own self-examination gives way, as was hinted in the previous section, to a momentary forgiveness in which we can hear not only the immediate wordplay on pane/pain, but reverberations between those words and the words "pun," "panic," and the important initiating circumstance, "punishment." The punishing slow pace of this self-criticism has yielded, despite impending panic, to the play of words, yet still within the prison of language.

Davie is too much the puritan to let himself off on a gaudy note of consolation or to let his poem become a pastoral. The final section, its tenth, is at once the most varied tonally, the most self-revealing, and the most moving. The play becomes self-punishment again as Davie "pummels his temples":

> "A shared humanity . . ."
> . . . .
> Surely,
> surely that means something.
>
> He knew too few in love,
> too few in love.
>
> That sort of foolish beard
> masks an uncertain mouth.
> And so it proved: he took
> some weird girl off to a weird
> commune, clutching at youth.
>
> Dear reader, this is not
> our chap, but another.
> Catch our clean-shaven hero
> tied up in such a knot?
> A cause of so much bother?
>
> He knew too few in love.

By the end of Larkin's poem, he knows many in love, in other words, all these newlyweds. But Davie knows, he claims, "too few." Yet detachment like Larkin's could hardly be ascribed to what Davie does know and has observed. In one of the most risky satiric caricatures I can imagine, Davie first skewers what appears to be a contemporary, perhaps the victim of a mid-life crisis, "clutching at youth." Then, he turns on himself, and plays on the doubleness he has presented throughout the poem to emphasize that in no way are we to mistake "our chap" for "another":

> Catch our clean-shaven hero
> tied up in such a knot?
> A cause of so much bother?

What adds to the chill of this portrait is its echo of one in a similarly structured and similarly emotional poem, from Davie's *Events and Wisdoms*, "After an Accident":

> Death is about my age,
> Smiling and dark, clean-shaven.

The "shared humanity" that must mean something has been glossed in numerous ways throughout the poem, as Davie responds to his possible carriage mates, to the remembered wisdom of grown-ups, to the traffic outside the train, to his wife and daughter, to the enviable position of Judith Wright who speaks for her nation, and to himself. Davie may not know what he means, but he does know how it feels to share the humanity of others, to be human. Larkin, on the other hand, does know what a shared humanity means, for others if not exactly for himself.

The line that is most moving and most ambiguous in this section is the refrain, "He knew too few in love." Michael Schmidt has read it simply as "He loved too few people." That is the reading that makes the most sense. Yet there are subtler overtones that are moving, too. In his knowledge of others there was not enough love. Of those he knew, too few were in love—even in love like the foolish bearded man with his weird girl. A commune might, indeed, be the sort of community Davie claims to know nothing of, a weird one as far as he can tell. The reproach implicit in this line is a Christian one. The Christian admonition, to love one's neighbor as oneself, moves Davie in many of his poems. No less does it here.

My distinction that Davie is a Christian poet and Larkin is not might seem strange only because the occasion of Larkin's poem is a Christian holiday. Yet Larkin's interest is in what characterizes the object of his affection; this has little to do with Christianity. In "Church Going," Larkin affirms the perpetuation of custom much as he does in "Show Saturday"—"Let it always be there." This is his theme in "The Whitsun Weddings" as well. Davie's concerns as a Christian are the salvation of his soul and the fellowship of his fellow human beings. It makes sense that as a Christian poet he would be distressed by the self's interference with these aims, especially as it uses language to obstruct them. Furthermore, it follows that he would find the lyric insufficient to express the obligations of a modern poet. "In the Stopping Train" tests the limits of the form, whereas "The Whitsun Weddings" goes beyond the form inadvertently and, perhaps, dubiously. It is tantalizing to imagine a form in which the achievements of both poems—the intensity of self-revelation and the understanding of the experience of others—are shared.

The Primal Storyteller

In 1980 Robert McDowell and I started a magazine called *The Reaper* which we dedicated to a revival of narrative poetry. We argued that narrative, which other literary forms continued to use effectively, had begun to disappear from poetry. Because it was the form that connected poetry to life as it was lived, it had to be revived. Narrative, we reasoned, provided meaning and made artistic demands that a poet avoided at his or her peril. Poets who did not have a story to tell should not be writing a poem. Our argument had some effect, but of course the renewed interest in narrative poetry was in the air. Others had realized how insular the lyric poem had become, how ineffective it was in communicating anything about life as it is lived. The notion of returning poetry to its roots as a medium of storytelling was catching on. Still, the significance of the story as a form and the way poetry can throw that form into high relief, these were nothing less than avant garde ideas for their time. They also led to some angry backlash and repudiation from the status quo, echoes of which linger today.

So it is with some satisfaction that I read the following claim by Stephen Jay Gould in the *New York Review of Books* (October 20, 1994):

> We are storytelling creatures and should have been named *Homo narrator* . . . rather than the often inappropriate *Homo sapiens*. The narrative mode comes naturally to us as a style for organizing thoughts and ideas.

And it is with particular interest that I read Bert O. States's new book, *Dreaming and Storytelling*, which confirms Gould's assertion

---

From *Hudson Review* (spring 1995).

and explores the relation of narrative to the unconscious. States's theory is that narrative is the basic form of literary art because it is rooted in the form of the dream, which itself is a reflection of life both as it is lived and as we desire it to be.

States begins by assuming that dreams are narratives and explains that, as such, the dream "is the narrative form in greatest need of examination." Dreams have been examined very thoroughly in this century, but not to States's satisfaction as literary or ur-literary forms. He picks a bone with Freud throughout his book, insisting that dreams are as irreducible to interpretation as any art form and affect our emotions in the same direct yet complicated way. He goes so far as to say that the Freudian censor does not distort dreams to disguise latent material, but that distortion is the means by which dreams express their imaginative meaning. To distort, he claims, is to make art.

A curious issue, however, in States's use of dreams as examples is that those he uses seem remarkably clear, remarkably coherent, remarkably narrative. Despite my predisposition to agree with States's argument, I sometimes wondered as I read if it was not just a bit too neat.

He handles what Freud called the uncanny in his first chapter, "The Problem of Bizarreness." Part of the strangeness of dreams, he says, is that what we dream "loses the status of the imaginary." And yet he also asserts that while dreaming we can imagine anything. By "anything" he probably means that the brain can imagine anything within the dreamer's ken, no matter how it is arranged. I have never dreamed of black holes, for example, and I doubt that Stephen Hawking would dream of my father. So, our brains cannot imagine just anything. Yet this limitation relates to the fact that, as States argues, our dreams are narrative because our lives are narrative. The bizarreness of dream narrative is also due to "the elasticity of fiction." Like a story, a dream can move from scene to scene without any overt or even logical reason. And yet he points out that, unlike a story, dreams "are authorless, unmediated by language, and they unfold intrepidly in a world no different from the waking world with respect to the authenticity of one's experience." While we experience dreams, often as characters within the narrative, we have no sense or are denied a sense of the author's controlling hand, even though that hand is our own. The bizarreness of dreams is due to our *unwilling* suspension of disbelief.

Yet who has not said to him or herself during a truly bizarre, usually frightening episode, this is or is not a dream? To help make his case, States appeals to the Russian Formalists, Victor Shklovsky in particular, and the theory of defamiliarization or estrangement. Defamiliarization is found, Shklovsky argued, "everywhere form is found." Therefore, dreams are bizarre not because they are formless, but because they are formal. Freud, too, has noted this. The difference between him and States is that States is interested in the form of the dream and not what it conceals.

States is at his very best when dealing with formal theories. In order to devise a way to think about distortion, so as to exclude the censor, he theorizes that "distortion is a form of classification" and has to do with the way the brain stores material. He makes an analogy between this method and the way in a dictionary one encounters totally unlike things in proximity simply because of their similar spellings. Opening a dictionary anywhere will offer up surreal juxtapositions, like nougat, nought, noumenon. Without distortion, States claims, "the dream would be radically limited in its powers of association." He paraphrases Descartes: "I think, therefore I distort; or, I think, therefore I make metaphors." Thus our memories are stored cheek by jowl in the brain's dictionary, and during the freedom of sleep, the author of dreams discerns likenesses among them that we would ordinarily dismiss.

Along with this process comes a sense that, States says, "dreams do not have beginnings and endings but seem rather to be all middle with occasional crises." To explain the narrative unfolding of a dream, he quotes Jean-Luc Godard, who said that his films all had a beginning, a middle, and an end, but not necessarily in that order. As for the mood of a dream, whether it be sexy or frightening, images that enter adapt to local conditions, as in natural selection. An aunt who is kindly in real life may, in a frightening dream, be a monster; or you may dream that you are sleeping with your mother, if the dream is about sex.

The reference to natural selection makes me wonder if natural selection is not itself a narrative that explains a process which may be hiding something else. It is possible that the narrative form of a dream may also be a distortion of the censor. States does not address these issues. As long as he keeps his argument on formal grounds, he is eloquent and persuasive, as in this key passage from his second chapter, in which he says that dreams are

> the first place stories were ever told—in the dreamwork, the primal storyteller preceding all fiction, the one story mechanism that produces a narrative structure that consciousness not only invents but inhabits at first hand.

The third chapter of the book, entitled "The Master Forms," includes a number of problematic areas. Instead of deferring to Jung, States considers the work of Formalists like I. V. Propp and his *Morphology of the Folktale* to argue that the narrative patterns of dreams follow many of the same patterns as literary narratives. He makes a provocative claim that dreams, while they are "the continuing saga of [our] imaginary life," tend not to be comic, and further, they rarely involve things or people with whom we are happy or about which or whom our emotions are resolved. From this claim he moves to Tolstoy's famous assertion at the beginning of *Anna Karenina*. Since all happy families are alike and need not be written about, States reasons, then happiness "has no narrative and therefore . . . requires no narrator." Presumably, in States's argument, happiness requires no dreamer, either. But Tolstoy did write about one happy family— the Rostovs, in *War and Peace*. And surely we can all recall dreams that made us very happy, that we did not wish to end. As for the comic in dreams, when my youngest daughter was little she invariably woke up in the morning giggling or laughing. While we may rarely find ourselves laughing in a dream, many a dream is based on the ironies we find in a joke. Again, Freud teaches us this. When States mentions in a footnote that "we do not dream in the style of a Robbe-Grillet novel or in the style of *Finnegan's Wake*," though he means to suggest that neither is essentially narrative in form, still exceptions spring to mind. Some dreams are populated by puns embodied in dramatic action or simply by physically represented words. The protagonist of

Robbe-Grillet's *The Voyeur* seems exactly like a dreamer caught watching himself in a dream.

Finally, departing from his narrative argument, States describes something he calls "the lyric dream" as "the self speaking to itself." Yet is this not true of every dream? In order to locate the author of the dream, the self behind the self who plans the dream narrative, States ends where Freud began. The primal storyteller is not the dreamwork; it is "desire."

Where States wants to end up is with an answer to his question, "Are dreams more like literature or more like the digestive system?" In his most detailed expression of his theory, he writes:

> The miracle of narrative formation can be explained by no other agency than some variation on the principle of scripted, schematic, or archetypal behavior, which we may think of as the grammar of memory in that it provides the combinational patterns with which memory can condense experience into narrative form. Thus the logic of storytelling is largely a matter of plagiarizing the world of social usage and abuse.

In other words, dreams are more like literature. But considering all he has argued and what he has left incompletely refuted, in other words, Freud's theory of dreams, I would have to say that dreams lie somewhere between literature and digestion. It may very well be that, as States says, "in the dream we are virtually at the site of pure creativity, where the associative process is not hampered by matters of comprehensibility or conceptuality." But for that very reason, we are not at the site where art is made or, I would venture, even in a totally analogous realm.

States admits early on in his book that our own dreams are rarely of much or any interest to others. W. H. Auden is on record as having said dismissively, "The subconscious is fundamentally boring." What the waking author does with the plagiarized world and what the primal storyteller does are, in the end, two very different things. When States suggests that a work of narrative art, poem or novel or short story, is its own interpretation, I am with him. But when he concludes that the same is true for the dream, I have to wonder. For if the primal storyteller, the author of dreams, the force that plans the narrative, is also desire, then whatever it is that desire wants is embodied in the dream and concealed there. We are back at Freud's thesis that the dream is the fulfillment of a wish, and that that wish may be distorted in the dreamwork because of its latent power, even its fearsomeness.

Perhaps Freud and States come closest when we think of that part of the dream Freud called its "navel," a part connected to the mystery of dreaming itself. States's formal argument may be taken as an explanation of that mystery. A formalist to the end, he provides a chart for his idea of how the dream becomes art: "life experience (desire)—dream—day dream—fiction and art." And he also creates a comparative list of how different critical methodologies—psychoanalytic, semiotic, phenomenological, structural, and deconstructive—would approach the narrative structure of dreams. In contrast to these critical approaches, he concludes that the purpose of dreams and stories is "not to produce meanings." As much as I am gratified by his thinking, I find myself changing from *Homo narrator* back to *Homo sapiens*, man who has and wishes to acquire knowledge. I want to know what it all means. That desire to know seems as primal as the desire to tell stories.

Throughout the Gospels Jesus relates his parables to a group of individuals who were not exactly selected for their imaginative abilities. Often when he tells them a story, they counter, "What do you mean?" And just as often he is reduced to telling them, in order to satisfy their unimaginative, literal-minded desire to know. But of course, it is always with another story.

Slip, Shift, and Speed Up

The Influence of Robinson Jeffers's Narrative Syntax

I wish I could change the second half of my title to "The Influence of Robinson Jeffers's Narrative *Energy*" in order to echo a book that I admire, Donald Davie's classic from 1955, *Articulate Energy: An Enquiry into the Syntax of English Poetry.* In fact, when I titled my essay, I had a portion of Davie's book in mind; for he theorizes that every sentence has a plot, even a tragic plot, and he derives this theory from H. M. McLuhan (Marshall McLuhan, to the rest of us), who suggested as much as he dwelt on certain couplets of Alexander Pope, like this one from "The Rape of the Lock":

> The hungry judges soon the sentence sign
> And wretches hang that jurymen may dine.

Davie notes that the couplet has a plot and a subplot and that its articulation depends on rhyme as much as on images.

Now, I know that this is beginning to get tangled. I would like to be as accurate as possible in what I am about to claim, while at the same time to honor my deceased colleague and fellow admirer of Robinson Jeffers, Donald Davie. I will, indeed, try to speculate on the nature of Jeffers's narrative energy as it originates in him and the poets I will try to associate with him; frankly, I think it comes from a moral impulse, which distinguishes him from his two great contemporaries, Robert Frost and Edwin Arlington Robinson, the other legs of the narrative

From *Jeffers Quarterly* 3, no. 4 (fall 1999): 10–23.

stool on which the curious but living tradition of modern narrative poetry rests. However, I will try to stick with the phrase "narrative syntax," not because of the plot of Jeffers's sentences, but because the syntax of his narrative verse is recognizable in a number of contemporary practitioners. It may be more recognizable than anything we hear in Frost or Robinson. The reasons are many and have in part to do with the division between free and formal verse in this country.

The first half of my title, "Slip, Shift, and Speed Up," comes from Jeffers's poem "Prescription for Painful Ends" and is a phrase he uses there to describe a rhythm of historical events; it is not meant in any way to be salutary or admiring, but to describe the pathetic manner in which modern nation-states try to regain their footing after slipping in some moral quagmire:

> The future is a misted landscape, no man sees
> clearly, but at cyclic turns
> There is a change felt in the rhythm of events, as when
> an exhausted horse
> Falters and recovers, then the rhythm of the running
> hoofbeats is changed: he will run miles yet,
> But he must fall; we have felt it again in our own life
> time, slip, shift, and speed-up
> In the gallop of the world. . . .

Nevertheless, I like the phrase and think it may help to describe the narrative syntax I hear in Jeffers and the contemporary poets I wish to discuss, because of its narrative energy, that moral impulse that leads Jeffers to create the metaphor and embed in it a narrative sequence of action, and because of its parallel structure. The poets I hope to bring before you share two aspects of Jeffers, then: the moral impulse of his storytelling verse and his means of narration—narrative energy *and* narrative syntax.

First, however, I would like to draw a clearer distinction between him and his great peers in the art of narrative verse, Edwin Arlington Robinson and Robert Frost. Here is a sonnet by Robinson.

The deacon thought. "I know them," he began,
"And they are all you ever heard of them—
Allurable to no sure theorem,
The scorn or the humility of man.
You say 'Can I believe it?'—and I can;
And I'm unwilling even to condemn
The benefaction of a stratagem
Like hers—and I'm a Presbyterian.

"Though blind, with but a wandering hour to live,
He felt the other woman in the fur
That now the wife had on. Could she forgive
All that? Apparently. Her rings were gone,
Of course; and when he found that she had none,
He smiled—as he had never smiled at her."

Robinson is motivated by the naturalist's desire to examine a slice of life and consider its reason for existence. In a sonnet like "Ben Trovato" he gives us a narrative almost as complicated as a novel by Henry James, complete with unreliable narrator and love triangle. The deacon conveys a story to us as juicy as gossip, a deathbed scene to rival the choosing of Jacob over Esau. We look on in amazement at the complexity of these human hearts, recognizing that this telling anecdote hints at social pressures created by the characters' beliefs about marriage and class, while at the same time giving us behavior that cannot be described by any "theorem" of society. In considering the way the wife disguises herself as her rival, we are, like our narrator, "unwilling even to condemn / The benefaction of a stratagem / Like hers," whether we are Presbyterians or not. All of our interest is in the way the sonnet holds this microscopic universe of haute bourgeois realism.

Robert Frost offers us something else, of course, something more, though in rather the same dimension of the relative, the pragmatic, in his narrative poems. Take the following, for example:

The buzz-saw snarled and rattled in the yard
And made dust and dropped stove-length sticks of wood,
Sweet-scented stuff when the breeze drew across it.
And from there those that lifted eyes could count
Five mountain ranges one behind the other
Under the sunset far into Vermont.
And the saw snarled and rattled, snarled and rattled,
As it ran light, or had to bear a load.
And nothing happened: day was all but done.
Call it a day, I wish they might have said
To please the boy by giving him the half hour
That a boy counts so much when saved from work.
His sister stood beside them in her apron
To tell them "Supper." At the word, the saw,
As if to prove saws knew what supper meant,
Leaped out at the boy's hand, or seemed to leap—
He must have given the hand. However it was,
Neither refused the meeting. But the hand!
The boy's first outcry was a rueful laugh,
As he swung toward them holding up the hand
Half in appeal, but half as if to keep
The life from spilling. Then the boy saw all—
Since he was old enough to know, big boy
Doing a man's work, though a child at heart—
He saw all spoiled. "Don't let him cut my hand off—
The doctor, when he comes. Don't let him sister!"
So. But the hand was gone already.
The doctor put him in the dark of ether.
He lay and puffed his lips out with his breath.
And then—the watcher at his pulse took fright.
No one believed. They listened at his heart.
Little—less—nothing!—and that ended it.
No more to build on there. And they, since they
Were not the one dead, turned to their affairs.

Is it right that the boy is in the lumberyard, doing a man's work? No, probably not, but there may be extenuating circumstances. It could be this is a family concern, with his sister doing the cooking, and besides he's a "big boy . . . though a child at heart." The accident that cuts his life short could have occurred as easily in the natural world as in the world of dangerous machines, although this is not the only Frost poem in which modern technology devastates a life, if you remember the early narrative "The Self-Seeker." The point of a Frost narrative, especially those we find in blank verse, is also to lift a section out of a life—which he has in common with Robinson—but without the naturalistic sense of determinism. What is happening is more open to interpretation; indeed, in his narratives contending views offer their imaginative responses to the fact of an event. In "'Out, Out—'" even the narrator interjects his belief that the tragedy might have been averted, if they had "call[ed] it a day" earlier. The boy, the sister, the doctor, the onlookers who turn away at the end, all have their particular stake in the meaning of the accident. What we are to make of it depends not on choosing a point of view but on recognizing how all of them contend. The blank verse of Frost's narratives may be his attempt to resolve moral ambiguity, as much as the more controlled forms of Robinson's ballads and sonnets may represent the determining factors of culture and society. I suspect that a free verse narrative of the contemporary variety that I will be talking about and that I think shows Jeffers's influence may be the paradoxical result of a moral clarity missing in Robinson and Frost.

So, how is Jeffers different? For one thing, he is not a relativist like Robinson or Frost. His stories are enactments of moral problems that have inevitable ends because the characters presented with these problems make the wrong choices. Admittedly, he, too, can be considered in the naturalist tradition, but I would put him there with Thomas Hardy, in his novels, in which characters choose badly, at times because they simply cannot help it. Jeffers's difference with Hardy (a writer of importance also to Robinson and Frost) is that Jeffers, one senses, is less forgiving of human weakness, because he is appalled at its tragic consequences. It may be that because of the moral drive or impulse to his narratives, we hear his influence more readily today than we hear the influence of Robinson or Frost. Moral clarity is part of his legacy. I hope the examples I am going to give you, from three contemporary poets, will persuade you that this is true. And because I don't want to lose track of my title, as much as I would like to flee its demands, I believe we will hear a kind of phrasing or expression in the contemporary narratives that I have chosen that recalls Jeffers more than Robinson and Frost, because of the nature of their syntax and free verse form.

First, let me consider Jeffers's *ars poetica*, "Apology for Bad Dreams," by focusing on the first of its four sections, a microcosm of his longer narratives.

Apology for Bad Dreams

1

In the purple light, heavy with redwood, the slopes drop
    seaward,
Headlong convexities of forest, drawn in together in the
    steep ravine. Below, on the sea-cliff,
A lonely clearing; a little field of corn by the streamside; a
    roof under spared trees. Then the ocean
Like a great stone someone has cut to a sharp edge and
    polished to shining. Beyond it, the fountain
And furnace of incredible light glowing up from the sunk
    sun. In the little clearing a woman
Is punishing a horse; she had tied the halter to a sapling at
    the edge of the wood, but when the great whip
Clung to the flanks the creature kicked so hard she feared
    he would snap the halter; she called from the house
The young man her son; who fetched a chain tie-rope, they
    working together
Noosed the small rusty links round the horse's tongue
And tied him by the swollen tongue to the tree.
Seen from this height they are shrunk to insect size.
Out of all human relation. You cannot distinguish
The blood dripping from where the chain is fastened,
The beast shuddering; but the thrust neck and the legs
Far apart. You can see the whip fall on the flanks . . .
The gesture of the arm. You cannot see the face of the
    woman.
The enormous light beats up out of the west across the
    cloud-bars of the trade-wind. The ocean
Darkens, the high clouds brighten, the hills darken
    together. Unbridled and unbelievable beauty
Covers the evening world . . . Not covers, grows apparent
    out of it, as Venus down there grows out
From the lit sky. What said the prophet? "I create good: and
    I create evil: I am the Lord."

As I proceed to consider this passage as free verse, let me acknowledge that I know how Jeffers regarded his double pentameter line and I know, too, that when the line contracts here, it is to a roughly pentameter line. Nevertheless, the poem is metrically freer than anything in Robinson and Frost, and its way of establishing rhythm derives not only from the English verse tradition, but from the repetition and parallelism we find in Biblical poetry and in Whitman. Notice the construction of the setting: "A lonely clearing; a little field of corn by the streamside; a roof under spared trees." And notice the way the narrator directs our gaze, after shrinking the humans "to insect size": "You cannot distinguish / The blood dripping from where the chain is fastened, / The beast shuddering; but the thrust neck and the legs / Far apart. You can see the whip fall on the flanks . . . / The gesture of the arm. You cannot see the face of the woman." The syntax here embodies action, imitates action, in which the animal's pain and the agent of that pain—the woman—though they cannot be distinguished, are united by what you can see: the whip, the gesture of the arm. In parallelism like this, details take on an equality. In Whitman, it is the democratic ideal of a self that contains all that it catalogues—these United States. In Jeffers, whom I once heard William Everson refer to as the dark nadir to Whitman's sunny zenith, the same syntax conveys moral judgment, its narrative energy. When section 1 ends, "What said the prophet? 'I create good: and I create evil: I am the Lord,'" I think we can infer that the good here is manifested in the "unbridled and unbelievable beauty" that "covers the evening world." The Lord has created it as surely as the evil taking place in the clearing. The two parts, good and evil, though unequal in value, are of equal weight. The recognition of that equality marks Jeffers as a tragic poet.

We may not see Jeffers's tragic dimension in the contemporary poems I am about to discuss, but we will sense his moral impulse, the source of his narrative energy and syntax. Here is a pair of poems from C. K. Williams's 1988 book *Flesh and Blood*.

The Mistress

After the drink, after dinner, after the half-hour idiot kid's
    cartoon special on the TV,

after undressing his daughter, mauling at the miniature
    buttons on the back of her dress,
the games on the bed—"Look at my pee-pee," she says,
    pulling her thighs wide, "isn't it pretty?"—
after the bath, pajamas, the song and the kiss and the telling
    his wife it's her turn now,
out now, at last, out of the house to make the call (out to
    take a stroll, this evening's lie),
he finds the only public phone booth in the neighborhood's
    been savaged, receiver torn away,
wires thrust back up the coin slot to its innards, and he
    stands there, what else? what now?
and notices he's panting, he's panting like an animal, he's
    breathing like a bloody beast.

The Lover

When she stopped by, just passing, on her way back from
    picking up the kids at school,
taking them to dance, just happened by the business her
    husband owned and her lover worked in,
their glances, hers and the lover's, that is, not the
    husband's, seemed so decorous, so distant,
barely, just barely touching their fiery wings, their clanging
    she thought so well muffled,
that later, in the filthy women's bathroom, in the stall, she
    was horrified to hear two typists
coming from the office laughing, about them, all of them,
    their boss, her husband, "the blind pig,"
one said, and laughed, "and her, the horny bitch," the
    other said, and they both laughed again,
"and *him*, did you see *him*, that sanctimonious, lying
    bastard—I thought he was going to *blush*."

I hope you could hear the way the action in both poems
comes in a series of parallel statements: "he's panting, he's
panting like an animal, he's breathing like a bloody beast" and
"so decorous, so distant, / barely, just barely touching their
fiery wings, their clanging." This sort of repetition is one way,
the primary way, free verse creates rhythm. The way it illumi-

nates and reveals the story, in a series of pulsing, parallel flashes, recalls Jeffers's own technique, his narrative syntax and energy.

And the story here, of sexual transgression that is like a violation of the landscape, is also reminiscent of Jeffers, although in this case, as in the other three poems I will discuss, the landscape is urban. The vandalized public phone in "The Mistress" that puts the unfaithful husband in a rage and the "filthy women's bathroom" in "The Lover" where the unfaithful wife hears the pair of typists give their choral denunciation of her are not directly the consequence of adultery, but they make us ponder its degradation. Both hang in the balance of the poems' parallel structure, with a weight equal to the husband's lies in "The Mistress" and the profane epithets in "The Lover." It is interesting to note that C. K. Williams in these and other poems speaks with a vehemence we sometimes hear in Jeffers, although Jeffers manages usually to keep a more Apollonian distance from what he disdains.

A poem that recalls Jeffers's cool, appraising, and yet judgmental detachment is Garrett Hongo's "Four Chinatown Figures" from his 1988 book *The River of Heaven.*

Four Chinatown Figures

In a back alley, on the cracked pavement slick with the
    strewn waste
of cooking oil and rotting cabbages, two lovers stroll arm in
    arm,
the woman in furs and a white lamé dress with matching
    pumps,
her escort in a tux casually worn—the black tie undone,
while she laughs, shaking her head back so the small,
mousse-stingered whips on the ringlets of her hair shudder
and dress sequins flash under the sore, yellow light of
    streetlamps.
Two dishwashers step from the back door of the Golden
    Eagle
arguing about pay, about hours, about trading green cards
with cousins for sex, set-ups with white women, for cigarettes
or a heated hotel room to sleep in on a dry, newspaper bed.

Bok-guai, they curse with their eyes, *Lo-fahn,* as the four
     nearly collide,
separate galaxies equal in surprise as they wheel to face each
     other.
The lawyer thinks little of these punks in T-shirts and Hong
     Kong jeans,
but the woman rhapsodizes, for no reason, in
     suspense/thriller prose—
slender and boylike, the bull's ring curl to their flimsy moustaches;
they must be cold in this dry, winter chill of late December in L.A.—
the sky a high velvet, indigo-to-black as it vaults, lazily,
from the city's fluorescent glow to the far azimuth
where the bear and huntsman drift casually into nothing.
Without jackets, the Chinese have bundled themselves in
     castoff,
cotton aprons stained with intricate patterns of lard and
     duck's blood
and wrapped like double-slings around their shoulders and
     folded arms.
Something grins on the face of the taller, fairer-complected
     one,
glints from his foxteeth, smolders in breathfog, camphor
     about to flare.
She tells herself, *Forget it, c'mon,* and, with a hooked finger,
snaps at the man's satin cummerbund. They turn away.
Without a gesture, in the greasy dark, the two Chonks turn
     away too,
back towards each other, and hear, quickening away behind
     them,
steps receding into the light din of street noise and sidewalk
     chatter.
The fair one says, audibly and in English, *Kiss me, white ghost,*
and, briefly staggered in the amniotic burst of light
from a passing tourist's flash, shrugs off his gruesome
     apron,
pulling out a pack of Gauloises, blue-wrappered, *especial,*
and strikes a match, holding it in the orange well of his
     hands
as, dragonlike, they both light up and puff, posed on a
     street vent,
hunching their thin shoulders and turning uptown against
     the wind.

The narrative syntax here appears to be more relaxed than in C. K. Williams's poems or "Apology for Bad Dreams." But the long, complicated sentences that describe the lovers in their leisurely, after-dinner walk end abruptly in the glare of those "sore, yellow" streetlamps. Then:

> Two dishwashers step from the back door of the Golden
>   Eagle
> arguing about pay, about hours, about trading green cards
> with cousins for sex, set-ups with white women, for cigarettes
> or a heated hotel room to sleep in on a dry, newspaper bed.
> *Bok-guai*, they curse with their eyes, *Lo-fahn*, as the four
>   nearly collide. . . .

Slip, shift, and speed up: repetition begins to pulse, the energy of the syntax brings two distinctly different moral forces together. After they meet, the syntax almost returns to a more leisurely, descriptive pace, as the Chinese pair become the focus, but the narration subtly maintains its parallel structure and repetition, as it considers these "separate galaxies equal in surprise as they wheel to face each other."

On the face of it, this poem represents what used to be called a clash of cultures, and the encounter between the expensive lovers, both indigenously associated with Los Angeles (one a lawyer from Wilshire Boulevard, the other a "city planner"), and the immigrant Chinese dishwashers looks like a literal rendering of such a clash. Although the figures meet each other in territory that by rights is Chinese, all four are identified as Chinatown figures, and, after all, Chinatown is as much a part of L.A. as the Wilshire district. And yet, the yuppie lawyer and his date, when they pause at the wishing well, which is decorated with figures from Chinese myth, behave in a way that looks awfully like sacrilege. The lawyer tosses in some worthless change and a piece of trash, and his date laughs at the act. The dishwashers, smeared with gore, appear then, as if they have been invoked, spirits of the desecrated well, eliciting contempt from the man and decadent daydreaming from the woman. In the end we also have to consider the urgent, even desperate concerns of the Chinese workers and the exotic foreignness of their curses alongside the exquisite attire and pursuits of the lovers. Insofar as the place itself exists as a reproach to the inhabitants, this is a landscape that recalls many in Jeffers, including the one at the beginning of "Apology for Bad Dreams." As the dishwashers light up their foreign cigarettes, they become native parts of a particular landscape, one that harbors dragons, embodiments of the moral impulse that shapes the poem and recalls Jeffers in the very way the human and the inhuman, the real and the mythic, the divine and the profane, confront each other.

I want to look at two more contemporary poems which I think recall Jeffers's moral impulse, his narrative energy, and his syntax, but first I would like to mention something that I noticed about some of these poems, after I chose them. In each, part of the poem's moral dimension depends on an animal or animals. The tortured horse in "Apology for Bad Dreams" and the pair of dragonlike dishwashers in "Four Chinatown Figures" serve in their respective poems as a moral focus. In C. K. Williams's two poems, this focus appears in the form of epithets. In "The Mistress," the frustrated husband is likened to "a bloody beast." And in "The Lover," the caustic typists refer to their boss as "the blind pig" and his wife as "the horny bitch." Granted we are seeing in each case examples of very old literary traditions, those of the fable and the allegory; still, it is striking to me that the following poem by Chase Twichell, "Aisle of Dogs," from her 1995 book *The Ghost of Eden*, should summon up Jeffers's own regard for animals in his poetry.

Aisle of Dogs

In the first cage
a hunk of raw flesh.
No, it was alive, but skinned.

Or its back was skinned.
The knobs of the spine

poked through the bluish meat.

It was a pit bull, held by the shelter
for evidence until the case
could come to trial,

then they'd put him down. The dog,
not the human whose cruelty

lived on in the brindled body,
unmoving except for the enemy eyes.

Not for adoption, said the sign.

All the other cages held adoptable pets,
the manic yappers, sad matted mongrels,
the dumb slobbering abandoned ones,

the sick, the shaved, the scratching,
the wounded and terrified, the lost,

one to a cage, their water dishes
overturned, their shit tracked around,

on both sides of a long echoey
concrete aisle—clank of chain mesh gates,
the attendant hosing down the gutters

with his headphones on, half-dancing
to the song in his head.

I'd come for kittens. There were none.
So I stood in front of the pit bull's
quivering carcass, its longdrawn death,

its untouched food, its incurable hatred
of my species, until the man with the hose
touched my arm and steered me away,

shaking his head in a way that said
Don't look, Leave him alone.
I don't know why, either.

The lines in Twichell's poem are short, no more than eight
syllables or four stresses usually, whereas those in Williams's and
Hongo's are long and recall Jeffers's double pentameter and
pentameter lines, respectively. It is possible that Twichell's are
short and theirs long because hers is a more imagistic poetry—
that is, more inclined to condense storytelling to as much as
the image alone can reveal. Nevertheless, in this poem, we
once again encounter the power of a narrative syntax that

brings Jeffers to mind. The way the pitbull's condition is revealed, the way the speaker takes in the surroundings, and the way she returns to regard the brutalized animal, until she is made to turn away, recall both the narrative syntax and the narrative structure of "Apology for Bad Dreams." Instead of Jeffers's grand and moving declaration, "'I create good: and I create evil: I am the Lord,'" we hear at the end of Twichell's poem the more modest, but just as moving, "Don't look, Leave him alone. / I don't know why, either." Human cruelty lives on, as the poet tells us, in the dog's body, and it will be the dog who is destroyed, after he serves a final human purpose in the trial of his violator; it will be the dog and not the human, she notes, who will die for this crime. I think we know what Jeffers himself would have written about such a thing. It is my hope that we can hear how he might have done so, by reading Twichell's poem.

Earlier I suggested that free verse, as we find it in Jeffers's narratives and the contemporary narratives I have been discussing, may be the result of moral clarity. This is the kind of notion that gets expressed in passing in a discussion like this, but lingers on to nag, because it sounds like a value judgment. I do not mean it to be one at all, since I do not think poetry in traditional English meters is in any way superior or inferior to American free verse. Still, I suspect that the traditional meters of English verse in their own clarity tend to resolve ambiguities, as they lend their authority to the most ambivalent argument. The writer of free verse may choose to base his or her authority on the urgency of the message. In the case of the narrative that shows Jeffers's influence, the structure of this message, as I have tried to argue, includes setting side by side, in a pattern of parallel structure, contending forces in a moral drama. The very rhythm and syntax of that drama, as it is narrated, derive from the clear idea that the forces, though of equal weight, are of differing value.

Let me illustrate with one more contemporary poem, this one by my colleague Kate Daniels, from a work in progress entitled *My Poverty*. The poem is called "Autobiography of a White Girl Raised in the South."

Autobiography of a White Girl Raised in the South

In any self-portrait from the 50s, you'd have to see the me
that was not me: the black girl trudging along the side of
   the road
while I whizzed past in my daddy's car. Or the not-me
girl in the bushes, peeing, while her mama kept watch
and I relieved myself inside, daintily, in the sparkling
   facilities
of the Southside Esso, labelled WHITES ONLY. All those
water fountains I drank from unthinkingly, all those lunch
   counters
where I disdained my lunch—she was there, around the
   corner
or outside, sipping from a Mason jar of tepid water her
   mama'd lugged from home,
eating her sandwiches of homemade biscuits and a smear of
   fat
on the bench for blacks, shadeless and dusty, on Broad
   Street in front of the depot.

From the beginning, then, there were always two: me and
   not-me.
The one I was, white and skinny, straight brown hair. And
   the one
I wasn't but could've been—that black or brown girl, hair
   coarser
than mine, eyes darker, skin gleamier and smooth, free of
   freckles.
I didn't even know where she lived, only saw her in public
when she stepped upon my granny's back porch with a
   paper bag
of okra, accompanying her mama selling turnips and
   tomatoes,
or her daddy, with his tools, come to sharpen the knives.
Then we looked at each other, I recall, hands behind our
   backs,
faces solemn and shy, our hair plaited, mine in one long,
   limp
twist, and hers in a dozen marvelous sprouts, each tied at
   the end
with colored twine. Now, I think it's odd, cruel even

I never put my hand out, showed off a toy, never asked her
   out
to my special place in my grandmother's yard, the powdery
   patch of gray dust
beneath the cherry tree, blossoms plopping down in tiny
   poofs
of air and color. There, cross-legged, knee to knee, we
   might've
touched each other and satisfied our terrible curiosity—
whether she, in fact, was just like me, and I, like her.
There, beneath the flowering tree, as the simple creatures
we were meant to be, the universe might have come to us
as once it was—various in its multitudes, full
of rich textures, interesting odors, a wide palette of color
   and hue.
There, we might have seen each other as the works of art we
   actually
were, might have understood the role of art, to explain the
   peculiar
state of being human, how it sometimes is a glorious thing
to be alive, to feel and see, how, at others, it's a crushing
weight, how one cannot exist without the other, how useless
any battle to divide the light from dark which can only
   coexist.
We might have seen how necessary we were each to the
   other,
how, separated by the bad laws and sick habits of the culture
   that produced us,
we were doomed to live bizarre, half-lives of racist lies.

Even now I see her toes, bare and curled in the powdery
   dust
and feel the envy that I felt for her going free of shoes,
my own toes twitching in my polished brogans. I see our
   hands reaching out
to fill with blossoms, dumping mine to her and hers to me.
And then I hear my granny's much-loved voice, calling
from the porch, to come away and go inside. She sends away
the not-me's daddy without a sale, and chastises me
   throughout our lunch
for what she calls "familiarity." And through the back
   screendoor,
I see the not-me girl, walking away behind her daddy, not

looking back, and I hear his voice, querulous, too, chastising
her, as well, for something bad, whatever it was we almost
   did
but didn't, finally, dare to do.

Not only does this poem, like the others, depend on a paral-
lel structure, in the small ways sentences are constructed and
the large ways the story is revealed, which we also find in Jef-
fers's narratives, but in one passage it echoes sentiments close to
those we find in many of Jeffers's poems:

> There, beneath the flowering tree, as the simple creatures
> we were meant to be, the universe might have come to us
> as once it was—various in its multitudes, full
> of rich textures, interesting odors, a wide palette of color
>   and hue.

Daniels tells a story about "the peculiar / state of being
human" in a society that deforms humanity. Even her choice of
the word "peculiar" has a Jeffersian quality, though the sub-
ject—racism—is not one he ever treated directly. And, of
course, that is not my point. My point is that Daniels's poem de-
rives its syntax from a narrative energy, the urge to tell a story in
verse, that embodies a moral imperative. It puts the experience
of a white child beside that of a black child, and weighs both in
the balance with the prejudice that separates them. This setting
side by side, making parallels in expression and in the structure
of the poem, has to make us think of the modern master of this
form.

When we encounter a contemporary narrative poem like
this one by Kate Daniels, and the ones by C. K. Williams, Gar-
rett Hongo, and Chase Twichell, free verse poems that tell sto-
ries with a moral clarity, in which opposing forces are set side
by side, in which the syntax itself reflects that opposition by its
parallel structure, a structure that by its very repetitive nature
creates the poem's rhythm and feeds on its narrative energy,
then the poet who comes to mind in the modern American tra-
dition of narrative poetry is Robinson Jeffers. It is not Edwin
Arlington Robinson, whose ballads and sonnets are like black

boxes with a voice inside. It is not Robert Frost, whose blank verse narratives, complete with live action and talking heads, are like documentary films. Jeffers took Walt Whitman's great free verse lyric, harnessed its power of reiteration for the purpose of narrative, and left this new form as part of his legacy to American poetry.

The Trace of a Story Line

One of the most intriguing parables of the Synoptic Gospels is the parable of the sower; Mark 4:3–9 is the simplest and most direct version of this story:

> Listen! A sower went out to sow and as he sowed, some seed fell along the path, and the birds came and devoured it. Other seed fell on rocky ground where it had not much soil, and immediately it sprang up, since it had no depth of soil; and when the sun rose it was scorched, and since it had no root it withered away. Other seed fell among thorns and the thorns grew up and choked it, and it yielded no grain. And other seeds fell into good soil and brought forth grain, growing up and increasing and yielding thirtyfold and sixtyfold and a hundredfold.

Completing his parable Jesus admonishes his listeners, "He who has ears to hear, let him hear." Pressed to explain the parable, he makes it clear that what the sower sows is the word, God's Word. His listeners are likened to kinds of soil. According to *The Interpreter's Bible*, the parable is, like all of Jesus' parables, "an earthly story with a heavenly meaning." But it is also another kind of story, one that exists apart from the meaning that Jesus gave it. It is an everyday fact, or was an everyday fact in a world where seeds were sown before ground was plowed. In this regard it is straight out of the Palestine Farmer's Almanac. Another exegesis in *The Interpreter's Bible* is that Jesus is speaking autobiographically. The sower's experience has also been his experience as a preacher.

Review of *The Other Side of the River* by Charles Wright and *Sweet Will* by Philip Levine, from *The Ohio Review* (fall 1986).

I want to examine in Charles Wright's *The Other Side of the River* and Philip Levine's *Sweet Will* how the story to which a meaning might be attached is presented as meaningful in itself, how the earthly story has been created without a heavenly meaning, although there is often in both poets a yearning for some meaning other than the natural fact of experience. In Philip Levine, particularly in his twelfth volume of poetry, we have a poet whose natural impulse is toward the significant anecdote, even the extended narrative. Charles Wright in his sixth book is a poet fully aware of what he has often suppressed in previous work—the narrative line—and who is now going so far as to call one poem "Two Stories." One important similarity between these two poets is a belief in the redemptive power of nature. For Levine, nature is that world poised in Romantic opposition to the city, where so much of his poetry is also set. For Wright, nature is all that is not human, the country that is better than the people, to paraphrase the quote from Hemingway that serves as epigraph to Wright's *Country Music: Selected Early Poems.* Often in the past Wright's poems have hurried away from the human milieu, but in *The Other Side of the River* they are at times crowded with people. Levine's poems have always been full of names, some attached to people and some anonymous in their chaste separation from an imaginable body, and *Sweet Will* is no exception. In both books, when name and place and time come together, story occurs. Why this happens is one question I would like to answer. The other is, What is the nature of meaning when the metaphorical form of a story is negated? Levine and Wright are also poets who return again and again to the denial, to insistence on the absence of anyone who might understand or care or remember, even to the insistence that they themselves do not always comprehend what they have written, either now or any longer. They invoke nothingness and its synonyms so often in their poetry that absence takes on an actual presence, like the Holy Spirit in a tongue of flame. To help me answer this second question I will draw on the critic Harriet Davidson's essay "Eliot, Narrative, and the Time of the World," which was published in the autumn 1985 issue of *The New England Review and Bread Loaf Quarterly.* In that essay she argues that narrative is actually a metonymic structure that expresses the finitude of human life and therefore makes possible a multitude of meanings and at the same time only one.

The Other Side of the River is divided into four parts. The first part is set primarily in the South with references to Italy, Montana, and Southern California, Wright's home when he was writing these poems. The poems are made up of blocks of long lines, including the staggered line that Wright perfected in the long title poem of *The Southern Cross*. "Lost Bodies," the first poem of *The Other Side of the River*, begins with the image of a Southern cross, a concrete one outside Wright's childhood home of Kingsport, Tennessee, carved with the words "GET RIGHT WITH GOD / JESUS IS COMING SOON." Time and place thus established, he relates the first of this volume's many stories:

> The cross was opposite Fleenor's Cabins below the hill
> On US 11W.
> Harold Shipley told me, when I was 12,
>   he'd seen a woman undressed
>
> In the back seat of a Buick, between two men,
>   her cunt shaved clean,
> In front of the motel office.
> They gave him a dollar, he said, to stick his finger up there.

Nothing else in this book is as blunt and brutal, though much is as mysterious. Furthermore, it is only this story that Wright himself admits makes any response, any attempt to make meaning, nearly impossible:

>   What can you say to that?
>   everything Jesus promised,
>
> (My five senses waiting apart in their grey hoods,
> Touching their beads,
>   licking the ashes that stained their lips)
>
> And someone to tell it to.

Part of this passage, as you can see, is an image of the poet's demurral and of his renunciation and petition. Still, the story has been told, and the reader is that someone he has found to tell it to.

"What can you say to that?" is the response elicited by many of the short but fully rounded tales Wright embeds in these poems. In an essay on Wright's poetry, Wyatt Prunty has suggested that in practicing the tall tale of the Southern variety, Wright has returned to his origins. That seems an accurate interpretation of Wright's temperament. The fixed location from which the mental traveler—or as Wright calls him, "the Pilgrim"—actually sets out in these poems is Southern California. He travels to the South, which is the past of childhood and adolescence; to Italy, which is the past of his young adulthood; and to Montana, a parallel place, a wilderness retreat, in the present. In all of these travels the personal account is told as a story, but not always as the tall tale that one boy might tell another to stand his hair on end.

At the heart of the second poem in the volume, "Lost Souls," is a theme Wright has treated elsewhere, the deaths of his mother and father:

> The last time I saw George Vaughan,
> He was standing in front of my father's casket at the laying out,
> One of the kindest men I've ever known.
>
> When I was 16, he taught me the way to use a jackhammer,
>   putting the hand grip
> Into my stomach and clinching down,
> Riding it out till the jarring became a straight line.
>
> He taught me the way a shovel breathes,
> And how the red clay gives away nothing.
> He took my hand when my hand needed taking.
>
> And I didn't even remember his name.

What can you say to that? The small failure of tact this records is magnified by the occasion and by the double death in forgetting the name of a father figure at the father's funeral. To consider this story in this way may help explain its emotional im-pact, but there is also an irrefutable factualness to it that is repeated at the end of the poem:

> A little curtain of flesh, Blake said,
> For his own reasons . . .
> And I had mine to draw it last night on the Wasatch Range
> And pull it back as the sun rose
> > over the north fork
> And blue weave of the Cumberlands.
> It was June again, and 1964 again,
> > and I still wasn't there
> As they laid her down and my father turned away,
> I still imagine, precisely, into the cave of cold air
> He lived in for eight more years, the cars
> Below my window in Rome honking maniacally
> > *O still small voice of calm . . .*

Whatever reasons he has to imagine himself drawing the night over the vast geographical middle of the American continent, still Wright has admitted us to their origin through the deft relation of a time, a place, and an event whose disunity he will never be able to bring together and atone for.

The book's third poem is a tour de force called "Lonesome Pine Special" in which Wright surveys the nation's landscape by means of a Whitmanesque cataloging of roads and highways: US 25E, US 23, Idaho 75, US 52, County 508, US 176, US 2, Montana 508, and one called Solo Joe after a legendary Montana prospector. Among the lives and landscapes he imagines and describes this story appears in the eighth section of the poem:

> Once, in 1955 on an icy road in Sam's Gap, North Carolina,
> Going north into Tennessee on US 23,
> I spun out on a slick patch
> And the car turned once-and-a-half around,
> Stopping at last with one front wheel on a rock
> > and the other on air,
> Hundreds of feet of air down the mountainside
> I back away from, mortal again
> After having left myself
> > and returned, having watched myself

Wrench the wheel toward the spin, as I'm doing now,
Stop and shift to reverse, as I'm doing now,
                    and back out on the road
As I entered my arms and fingers again
Calmly, as though I had never left them,
Shift to low, and never question the grace
That had put me there and alive, as I'm doing now . . .

There are two other stories Wright tells in which grace, questionable or unquestionable, appears to be involved. One of them is in the next poem, "Two Stories," and tells of how as a boy sleepwalking one night on a camp out he was impeded from falling off a cliff when the live body of a bear stopped him, woke him, and he was able to make his way safely back to camp. The other story comes in the second part of *The Other Side of the River,* in the poem "Italian Days," and recounts a near accident in a helicopter whose engine cut out "thousands of feet above the Brenner highway" so that Wright, then in U.S. Army Intelligence, nearly became "a squib / in the *Stars & Stripes.*"

Wright himself would be the first to say that these are the events of anyone's life, that any one of us could relate similar anecdotes of times when, but for the grace of God, our lives would have ended before we had fully lived them and perhaps understood them. The sleepwalker in "Two Stories" claims that after he made it back to his tent and to sleep he "never told anyone / Till years later when I thought I knew what it meant, / which now I've forgot." Lest we too easily link this story, as I have done, with other testimonies of grace, it is necessary to examine the second story of "Two Stories." Admitting that this story is questionable, Wright tells of a friend "who'd killed a six-foot diamondback about seven o'clock in the morning" and chopped its head off. That evening when he reaches in a sack to show a friend the dead snake the headless stump strikes his wrist hard enough to bruise it "for a week." What can you say to that? Here is what Wright says:

It's not age,
        nor time with its gold eyelid and blink,
Nor dissolution in all its mimicry
That lifts us and sorts us out.

It's discontinuity
        and all its spangled coming between
That sends us apart and keeps us there in a dread.
It's what's in the rear-view mirror,
               smaller and out of sight.

Without a head the serpent cannot bite its tail and roll into proverb or into a Yeatsian cosmology where "all the barrel-hoops are knit." Discontinuity is a serious and elusive thing to demonstrate through the necessary continuity of narrative. But it is the inexplicable, the other side of the river, that Wright always aims to present us in his poetry. That thing we call grace is, finally, an utter mystery:

I'm 15 again, and back on Mt. Anne in North Carolina
Repairing the fire tower,
Nobody else around but the horse I packed in with,
           and five days to finish the job.
Those nights were the longest nights I ever remember,
The lake and pavilion 3,000 feet below
              as though modeled in tinfoil,
And even more distant than that,
The last fire out, the after-reflection of Lake Llewellyn
Aluminum glare in the sponged dark,
Lightning bugs everywhere,
         the plump stars
Dangling and falling near on their black strings.

These nights are like that,
The silvery alphabet of the sea
            increasingly difficult to transcribe,
And larger each year, everything farther away, and less clear,
Than I want it to be,
        not enough time to do the job,
And faint thunks in the earth,
As though somewhere nearby a horse was nervously pawing
   the ground.

           "The Other Side of the River"

Although he has said with a tongue-in-cheek humor he rarely displays, "There is so little to say, and so much time to say it in," here Wright brings the urgency of that fifteen-year-old working high and alone into the present. There is not enough time to do the job. Again and again throughout The Other Side of the River, story is used to underscore this fact, the fact of finitude, either of the past, which memory represents poorly, or of the future, which will terminate for sure. The time that deludes us by seeming so vast is the present, and the little we have to say also faces us with our limitation, the small space of our lives, the shrinkage of our urgent stories.

I will come back to *The Other Side of the River* when I examine Wright's and Levine's use of negation. Now I want to compare the way in which Philip Levine employs his characteristic narrative style in *Sweet Will.*

It may have come earlier, but some time during the composition of *One for the Rose,* the 1981 volume that preceded his *Selected Poems,* Philip Levine decided that he did not have to be Philip Levine anymore. That is to say, he seemed to conclude that identity, that frozen form, could be changed by recharacterization, just as life could be given symmetry by narrative. Thus, in *One for the Rose,* there is the poem "I Was Born in Lucerne," which begins, "Everyone says otherwise," but insists to the end, "I breathed the truth. I was born in Lucerne." Directly before it in the book comes the poem "My Name," in which the letters of Levine's name are invested with separate meanings, especially the *n,* "one letter that says / 'nothing' or 'nuts' or 'no one' or 'never' / or 'nobody gives a shit.' But says it / with style. . . ." Of course, Levine has never ceased being Levine; he has simply fleshed himself out further, more exotically, more imaginatively, and *Sweet Will* continues this elaboration. To do this, as he always has, Levine uses narrative like a great talker and liar.

There are sixteen poems in *Sweet Will,* and narrative is central to each. This is partly due to temperament, just as Wright might be said temperamentally to prefer the epiphany, the moment of radiant illumination, to the mundane and pedestrian buildup. Where Wright is a mental traveler or represents himself as such, Levine depicts himself physically in motion—walking, driving, riding, and in one case sailing—toward the moment of utterance. The volume opens with "Voyages," which appears to tell about life on Lake Erie aboard one of "the old lake boats" whose captain drank—one of the stupid jobs, perhaps, that Levine's biographical note often refers to: "Enormous in his long coat / Sinbad would take the helm and shout out / orders swiped from pirate movies." Among the realistic details the name "Sinbad" calls the story itself into question. The answer shuttles back and forth between levels of irony and fantasy. "Salts and Oils," next in the book, offers a similar double exposure as it catalogues a series of adventures and meals, beginning, "In Havana in 1948 I ate fried dog / believing it was Peking duck. Later, / in Tampa I bunked with an insane sailor / who kept a .38 Smith and Wesson in his shorts." The poem unfolds as quickly as imagination can carry it; so masterful has Levine become with his Scheherazaderie that it ends both convincingly and outlandishly:

> One quiet morning
> at the end of my thirteenth year a little bird
> with a dark head and tattered tail feathers
> had come to the bedroom window and commanded
> me to pass through the winding miles
> of narrow dark corridors and passageways
> of my growing body the filth and glory
> of the palatable world.

The most highly charged and beautiful word in the language is the word *once*. The problem for any storyteller is how, having uttered that word, to end. Levine states in the book's central poem, "Poem with No Ending," that his poems "never end, they run on / book after book, complaining / to the moon that heaven is wrong / or dull, no place at all to be." Yes, indeed, but in the sleight-of-hand of the narrative line, Levine shows very well not only how to end but what we expect by an end and what we hope for when we see that the beginning is not satisfactory. Having, in the first two poems, played with cause and effect, with sequence and apparent fact, in the third poem, "Those Were the Days," Levine presents himself in a world that the readers of the never-ending poems of Philip Levine will know immediately to be out-of-character:

The sun came up before breakfast,
perfectly round and yellow, and we
dressed in the soft light and shook out
our long blond curls and waited
for Maid to brush them flat and place
the part just where it belonged.
We came down the carpeted stairs
one step at a time, in single file,
gleaming in our sailor suits, two
four year olds with unscratched knees
and scrubbed teeth. Breakfast came
on silver dishes with silver covers
and was set in table center, and Mother
handed out the portions of eggs
and bacon, toast and juice.

One expects the end at any moment in this poem, and it comes
in the form of a poetic turn, a volta, that is a transformation:

My brother flung
his fork on the polished wooden floor
and cried out, "My eggs are cold, cold!"
and turned his plate over. I laughed
out loud, and Mother slapped my face,
and when I cleared my eyes the table
was bare of even a simple white cloth,
and the steaming plates had vanished.

This is the broken spell of many another myth and fairy tale,
with parallels in the punishment of Tantalus, in Keats's "La Belle
Dame Sans Merci," and even in Christina Rossetti's "The Goblin
Market." These parallels exist because metamorphoses are plea-
surable to Levine (and he makes them so to us), and like all
such archetypal tales, they exist beyond any attempt to edify
them, to apply meaning to them. The magical realm vanishes,
as we knew it would have to since this is Philip Levine's poem:

My brother said, "It's time," and we
struggled into our galoshes and snapped
them up, slumped into our pea coats,
one year older now and on our way

> to the top through the freezing rains
> of the end of November, lunch boxes
> under our arms, tight fists pocketed,
> out the door and down the front stoop,
> heads bent low, tacking into the wind.

The ending of "Those Were the Days" also marks the ending for this sort of playfulness in this sad and haunted book. There were more poems of this sort in *One for the Rose*. *Sweet Will* is haunted by presences from the past—the father lost in 1933, the poet's brother, and the poet himself as a young man. There are places, too—California, Detroit, and Europe, with some references to Spain but also settings in Italy. If there is a singular purpose to the book, and I think there is, it is to discover what has made Levine the poet we recognize.

After the first three poems Levine's use of narrative, like Wright's, becomes more an isolated instance, stripped to the mystery of fact, so that in "Look" a son and mother on different shifts at a factory are imagined greeting each other as they pass on the street. In "The Present," a poem in five parts, memories of work as a teenager include the poet's brother, the kindness of a fellow worker named Baharozian, and an old man's fall from a high pallet where he slept in a warehouse. The title poem returns to the subjects and even the apparent form of poems in *Not This Pig* and *They Feed They Lion*. It sharply emphasizes the difference between past and present; I will return to it. In "Poem with No Ending" we see Levine testing the unadorned power of narrative. Two of the stories he tells stand out for comment. One story in part six of the poem is about work, this time as a mover some thirty years before:

> In another house an old man summoned
> me to a high room. There before us
> was a massive steamer trunk full
> of books he could take back home
> to Germany now he could return.
> Tolstoi, Balzac, Goethe, all
> in the original. Oh yes, I knew
> the names, and he called down
> to his wife, how wonderful!

This boy knows the names. He brought
the top down carefully, turned the key,
and stepped back, waiting for me
to carry it down three flights
by myself and offered me money
when I couldn't budge it, as though
I'd been pretending. This boy,
this American, in his pressed
work clothes, surely he could do it,
surely there was a way, if only
I would try. I left him shaking
his great head and passed his wife
on the stairs, a little brown mouse
of a woman laughing at such folly.

There are words here, like "this American" and "such folly," that
invite us to hunt for symbols, but there is also at the core a sim-
ple irreducible fact that has been placed in parallel correspon-
dence to other similarly mysterious events whose meaning
might be called hermetic. Two sections later there is an account
of how walking "in the high mountains of the West" the poet
and his youngest son had "descended slowly for a mile or more
/ through a meadow of wildflowers / still blooming in July."
They wander on, and the father listens to the son talk of animals
"with the gift of speech." They enter a thick forest, and the fa-
ther realizes that he has lost the way. They rest in a clearing. Fi-
nally the father hits on an idea:

I bet him he couldn't lead us back
the way we'd come through the dark
bear woods and across the great plain
and up and down these hills.
A dollar? he said. Yes. And talking
all the way, he took the lead,
switching a fallen branch before him
to dub this little tree as friend
or a tall weed as enemy, stopping once
to uproot a purple wildflower for me.

The faith the father puts in his little boy is similar to the faith
the narrator must put in his tale. He must believe it will lead

him back, that its passage will be self-evident between *once* and *the end.*

Because Levine has made that journey so often and so successfully may be the reason why in "Last Words" he tries to imagine a death he escaped, and in so doing imagine death itself. This is a pursuit of Wright's, too, and for Wright it has to do with a palpable desire for transcendence. This may also be Levine's aim, but there is something else, closer to what I hope to conclude about both poets' use of narrative. Imagining himself to have been struck down somehow beside a country road he writes:

> I did not rise.
> A wind or a stray animal or a group
> of kids dragged me to the side
> of the road and turned me over
> so that my open eyes could flood heaven.
> My clothes went skittering down
> the road without me, ballooning
> out into any shape, giddy
> with release. My coins, my rings,
> the keys to my house shattered
> like ice and fell into the mountain
> thorns and grasses, little bright points
> that make you think there is magic
> in everything you see. No, it can't
> be, you say, for someone is speaking
> calmly to you in a voice you know.

We do know that voice, and because we do and because we insist on the nonfictional authenticity of the poem's speaker, we might legitimately withhold belief when he immerses himself in the imagination of his death. The reader that Levine imagines negates this story, terminates it, just as the poem's title is negated (it is not the last poem of the volume), and by doing so invests it with meaning or, at least, makes meaning possible.

The negation Levine imagines and puts in the mouth of his reader here is an act in which he himself engages in almost every poem. Such negation can be interpreted tonally. In "Salts and Oils," after detailing his adventures in post–World War II America, Levine admits:

> These were not
> the labors of Hercules, these were not
> of meat or moment to anyone but me
> or destined for story or to learn from
> or make me fit to take the hand
> of a toad or a toad princess or to stand
> in line for food stamps.

The self-deprecating irony of this is clear, but some of these demurrals are refuted in part by the sometimes magical or fanciful events of the poem, including the already quoted passage that begins, "One quiet morning." Levine concludes that we have been told all this finally because "it pleases me." Once again, there is self-deprecation in that remark and sleight-of-hand, too.

This handling of illusion, as I have implied, occurs in the metamorphosis of the story in "Those Were the Days." The ridiculous luxury Levine imagines for his brother and himself, four-year-olds with unscratched knees, is negated by age and by the change of situation. The impossibility of the former story is made clear by the contrasting one, whose terms are believable because we know the world of Levine's poems and because the hardship, coming at us brutally and suddenly, startles us into belief. The point is that in poising these opposites against each other, Levine makes the form of each of them clearer.

In a way Levine's use of negation implies its opposite always, as in "Look":

> They will pass, mother and son,
> on the street, and he will hold
> her straight, taut body for
> a moment and smell the grease
> in her hair and touch her lips
> with his, and today he will not
> wonder why the tears start and
> stall in her eyes and in his.
> Today for the first time in
> his life he will let his hands
> stray across her padded back
> and shoulders, feeling them

give and then hold, and he will
not say one word, not *mother*
or *Ruth* or *goodbye.*

And to the reader, the one he exhorts to look at these two ac-
tors in the poet's memory, altogether alive there in the illusion
of narrative, he says, "Go ahead and look! . . . No one's blaming
you." That is a "no one" fully as real as any "someone" or as the
"I" of the poet himself. What such a negation does, however, is
to isolate the moment, slash and burn everything around it, so
that it has or attains a kind of chastity, even purity, as fact. It
could be that this is a chastening of the sentimental, Levine's
way of keeping himself and the reader honest.

As I indicated before, the difference between the past and
the present is clearly distinguished by the book's title poem.
This poem could be seen as a paradigm of the way Levine's
other poetic talents—for physical detail, for setting, for realism
of character, for native dignity—affect his use of narrative:

> The man who stood beside me
> 34 years ago this night fell
> on to the concrete, oily floor
> of Detroit Transmission, and we
> stepped carefully over him until
> he wakened and went back to his press.

One of the older workers assures the young Levine that the man
will get up "at his own sweet will." The man's story takes six stan-
zas to tell, and in the telling much more is told. When Stash
rises again he addresses his fellow workers:

> "Nigger, Kike, Hunky, River Rat,"
> but he gave it a tune, an old tune,
> like "America the Beautiful." And he danced
> a little two-step and smiled showing
> the four stained teeth left in the front
> and took another suck of cherry brandy.

The poem's last four stanzas insist on the pastness of all this
through the use of negation, which is insisted on as truth: "In

truth it was no longer Friday. . . . In truth all those people are dead. . . . And in truth I'm not worth a thing. . . . Not worth a thing!" In truth the world that "runs on and on at its own sweet will" is demarcated by two great negations, eternal periods of darkness, and in one way or another every story is an imitation of this span.

This may seem to be a cause of despair. It may even be the reason that Levine, who is not a desperate poet, so often responds to his own storytelling by negating it, as if by implying that it never happened he could keep it from happening, like his imagined death in "Last Words." To avoid the suggestion that either Levine or Wright is anywhere so superficial, however, I would regard Levine's "The House," which precedes "Last Words," as the epitome of his skepticism at its deepest. Although he can imagine a wedding taking place "in the stuffy front room" of the house and the arrangements infusing the gray place with a sparkling anticipation, in fact, "no one is going in or out." The poem that is only a house or the house that is a poem first has a locked door and is vacant. Nothingness and all it implies have for Levine, and for Wright, too, as much substance as their opposite. I think this is made clear throughout Levine's work in poem after poem. The most recent expression of it is in "rain," the third and last section of "Jewish Graveyards, Italy," the last poem of the book:

> I can
> stand under an umbrella, a man
> in a romance I never finished
> come to tell the rain a secret
> the living don't want and the dead know:
> how life goes on, how seasons pass,
> the children grow, and the earth gives
> back what it took. My shoes darken.
> I move from one cluster of stones
> to another studying the names
> and dates that tell me nothing I
> hadn't guessed.

This passage includes the tonal adjustments the poet makes to avoid sentimentality, but the larger issue is very much present.

Here nothing is what exists outside the poem, and its representative to the poem is narrative as Levine uses it.

This is how Charles Wright uses narrative, too, but with a difference. Wright's negations, as I have said, proliferate in his poetry as much as Levine's do. Because the fundamental form of his poems is not narrative—so much so that when he employs narrative one detects a significant difference in the matter of his poetry—there is also a more emphatic sense to Wright's treatment of nothingness. It truly is imperiling, and against it there may be little that can be done.

To return to the poem "Two Stories," I want to look again at Wright's own response to his tall tale about sleepwalking. He had never told anyone about it "till years later when I thought I knew what it meant, / which now I've forgot." What is missing? Apparently there was a time and a place and presumably at least one other person listening when Wright related this story and its meaning. So he says. But now he tells it and claims he has forgotten that meaning. Imagine Jesus turning on the disciples and saying to them, "Figure it out for yourselves!" or "I can't remember why I told that one." But my facetiousness is merely to suggest that a readily applicable meaning is not what Wright seeks. He wishes to express whatever it is that negates meaning. In this case, it is forgetfulness. Wright embodies his negations in other ways, too. Along with forgetfulness there are darkness, emptiness, and nothingness. Where Levine negates in order to strip the story of sentimentality and to isolate it in its pure factualness, Wright does so usually to understand negation itself. Again, in "Two Stories" he disqualifies age, time, and dissolution until he hits on what he believes is the nature of negation: "It's discontinuity."

Wright's use of narration enables him to characterize experience in the past, the present, and the future always in relation to what is missed. Thus in "Italian Days," where he remembers his youth in the Southern European Task Force:

> On alternate Sundays we'd drive to Soave and Asolo,
> Padova and the Euganean Hills,
> Always looking for the event,
>   not knowing that we were it.

This not knowing is the anxiety and glory of youth, for, as Wright goes on:

> At the end of the last word,
> When light comes walking across the lake on its hands,
> And nothing appears in the mirror,
>   or has turned to water
> Where nothing walks or lies down,
> What will your question be,
> Whistling the dogs of mold in, giving them meat?
> And what will it profit you?
>
> No thought of that back then. . . .

No, of course not, for had there been "thought of that back then," there would have been no youth, none of the experience that rises again and again from the darkness of memory.

One reason Wright gives us for ransacking his past comes at the end of the first poem of the fourth part of *The Other Side of the River*, "Arkansas Traveller" (readers of Wright should hear the echo of "Delta Traveller," in *Bloodlines*). He recalls his great-grandfather's emigration from Austria, his service in the Confederate army, then settling in Little Rock where Wright himself would spend his childhood summers with his grandparents. The poem concludes:

> Knot by knot I untie myself from the past
> And let it rise away from me like a balloon.
> What a small thing it becomes.
> What a bright tweak at the vanishing point, blue on blue.

I will risk claiming there is a pun in "Knot by knot" on "not by not." Thus Wright's use of memory is to purge himself of memory, to release himself from the past, to negate it. But that is a task, thankfully, he will never finish.

The book's last poem could be read as a satire of people without a history. Called "California Dreaming," it echoes the sentiment of more than one popular song:

We are not born yet, and everything's crystal under our feet.
We are not brethren, we are not underlings.
We are another nation,
        living by voices that you will never hear,
Caught in the net of splendor
            of time-to-come on earth.
We shine in our distant chambers, we are golden.

These figures may be "apotheosizic," but they are also part of what makes Wright ask himself "what in the hell I'm doing out here." Whatever Wright has to do is not yet done, not accomplished by *The Other Side of the River*, and this sense of the incomplete, the unfinished, is what is represented by the Aristotelian middle of all stories. The book's penultimate poem, "Looking at Pictures," describes Wright in his study looking at "photographs / And reproductions of all I've thought most beautiful. . . ."

        Rothko has a black-on-red
    Painting
    . . . .
    I'd sink through flat on my back
    Endlessly down into nothingness . . .

    But not now. Not now when the hound of the Pope's men
    Is leaping, not now
                when the banner of St. George
    Dragontails out of the sky. Not now
    When our fathers stand in their riding boots, arms crossed,
    Trying to tell us something we can't quite hear,
                    our ears jugged like Kafka's.
    The devil eats us, I know, but our arms don't touch his neck.

The tension in the poetry of Charles Wright is just this recognition of what he calls the "emptiness" that is "the beginning of all things" and its opposite, another negation, that seduces us without our will or compliance, to which our response throughout our lives is "Not now." This tension is also the factor that raises Wright's poetry, in my estimation, to greatness.

    Much of what I have tried to express in this essay is better put by the critic Harriet Davidson in the essay I referred to earlier in this essay. Her essay is drawn from her book, *T. S. Eliot and Hermeneutics: Absence and Interpretation in "The Waste Land."* Davidson points out that in Eliot's great poem there are a number of narrative segments that no metaphorical analysis of the poem has ever really explained. She argues that they are, in fact, mimetic of temporality and as such "opaque to interpretation," much as are the events, the disunified moments, of our lives. Within Eliot's poem they are a relief from the barren symbolic landscapes of the lyric passages, yet they also represent a grim alternative to a potentially beautiful nature, for they insist on life's finitude. Finally, paraphrasing Heidegger, Davidson states, "In order to have possibility, we must have finitude."

This is where I would like to conclude my own discussion of *The Other Side of the River* and *Sweet Will.* I believe this is what Charles Wright and Philip Levine, very similar and distinctly different poets, understand about narrative, too. Their similarity and difference are underscored by the use of the river, an ancient symbol of time, in the titles of their books. Levine draws his from Wordsworth's sonnet of 1803, "Composed upon Westminster Bridge," to depict time's movement through the present. Wright's title, as I have remarked earlier, shows him concerned with what is beyond time or, rather, with what faces it from the other side of our own regard. All that we can see and tell about is our portion of the river. Wright and Levine know that this is what narration means. It is partly for this that they are valuable poets. They would not have asked for an explanation of the parable of the sower, aware as they are in their own poetry that the meaning of a story is manifold and one.

On Either Side of the Water

The English poet Herbert Lomas's *Selected Poems* is the kind of book you can open anywhere to find a gem that makes you wonder how reputations are established. I do not think Lomas is a poet American readers know, even though there has been a general slowdown of poetry imports from across the Atlantic (just as there has been a drag on exports from this country to the United Kingdom). But checking the biographies of poets of his generation in *The Columbia History of British Poetry,* I find he is not mentioned among those born in the 1920s. Too bad, because the readers who do not know about Lomas are missing a unique voice and point of view, a method of perception and expression that I, for one, have not heard in English verse since Stevie Smith died. Lomas, who entitled his first book *Chimpanzees Are Blameless Creatures,* writes about love and sex like this, in the poem "Something, Nothing and Everything":

> There was nothing between us
> then something took off her dress
> something took off my shirt
> something took off her brassière
> and something took off my trousers
> then something took off her knickers
> something took off my pants
> there was nothing between us
> we touched each other
> everything was touching between us
> we kissed each other
> there was something between us
> then everything entered her body

From *The Hudson Review* (autumn 1996).

> there was everything between us
> there was nothing between us

Lomas is as interested in cognition as he is in feeling. Yet he manages, through sheer oddness and originality of expression, to make feeling as important as cognition. His *Selected* begins with the poem "Notes on Wittgenstein," the last two lines of which ask, "Is it you I love or myself? / And are roses red in the dark?" His poetry is haunted by love, mainly erotic and theological. As for the latter, he is down to earth, trying to come to terms with the idea of Christian charity, and here, too, he is reminiscent of Stevie Smith. But there is another important influence, rare in contemporary British poetry, and that is the great eighteenth-century realist George Crabbe, fellow citizen of Lomas's home, Aldeburgh, in Suffolk. A stranger combination of predecessors would be hard to find anywhere. "St Martin-in-the-Fields" begins, "City churches aren't always easy / to pray in," and focuses with Crabbe's cold eye on the London milieu, then makes the following turn:

> Yet here bums in a blue-chinned Greek-looking worshipper,
> pockets stuffed with evening newspapers, coat
> flapping, and grabs his God by the throat:
> he prays precipitately, wagging his head—a pew-gripper
> pointing out to an old employer—what?
> Is it horses? A tip flopped? A reproach or not?
>
> And suddenly I'm in it: his grace has snatched
> me out: over the altar the angels' faces
> break the wood: they're reaching down with fact,
> listening, embracing, swooping, and I'm hatched:
> a broad white shell of completeness
> has widened and cracked:
> I'm open to sweetness.

It is rare to find Crabbe "open to sweetness," though he fully understood its source and possibility. But it does seem like a resolution Stevie Smith might have come to. Here the remarkable combination of gritty realism and quirky grace is typical of Lomas alone.

The book includes poems from Lomas's seven previous collections. My only complaint is that we have to guess which poems are from which book, and they are not arranged chronologically. This may not be a bad thing, since, as I have said, this is a book to open anywhere. The poems do appear to be arranged thematically. There is a group of poems based on Lomas's upbringing in Todmorden, Yorkshire, stressing the warmth and humanity of the place. "This valley's beautiful not picturesque," he begins, and later fondly remembers "the happiness, the wine, the big dinners, the talk." And there is a long series, probably his masterpiece, called "Letters in the Dark," set, the subtitle tells us, at Southwark Cathedral. He echoes the vulnerability of an American poet like James Wright when, imagining his death, he admits, "I'll need some friends who've been there when I go."

One of Lomas's strengths is the elegy. He is gifted with a deadpan sympathy that makes him a curiously compelling threnodist. "Elegy for Robin Lee" begins, "People get very upset / when you take your life." This approach is especially touching when taken with his own, recently deceased spouse, Mary Lomas, to whom the book is dedicated. The last poem, "The End," addresses her:

> It was sad to see your sheets
> revolving in the washing machine
> . . . .
>
> It's a privilege to know you're prettier
> with your clothes off than on,
>
> which isn't true of everyone. . . .
>
> Our eyes are in touch with
>
> transcendence. Some day
> shall we be together?

Herbert Lomas's is a fresh, original voice. I hope he will gain readers on both sides of the Atlantic with this book.

Unlike Lomas, Charles Tomlinson is very well known on both sides of the Atlantic. *The Columbia History of British Poetry* notes that he has had teaching stints in the United States as well as Britain. Those who know his work are aware that it reflects an interesting combination of values associated with The Movement—a classical formalism and precision—along with the influence of William Carlos Williams. In *Jubilation,* his seventeenth book in a career that spans forty years, he passes back and forth between the short, sinewy line of Williams and a crisp iambic pentameter, occasionally rhyming in both forms.

Landscape is his preferred subject. There are scenic poems about Gloucestershire, near the banks of the Severn, where he currently lives, and Italy, Portugal, and Japan. The following short poem, "Asolo," seems typical of his approach to the picturesque:

> Fountains of limestone, limestone colonnades
> > Reverberating like wells, porticoes of shade
> And against the sky the dark of cypresses:
> > Browning brought them back from Tuscany
> To stand against the sunset. Terraces
> > Could not mark the gradation of a hill
> More exactly than their ranks, and when the sun
> > Climbs down behind them, one
> By one they offer it their stair
> > To steady its descent then disappear.

History is often added like a spice, as it is with the reference to Browning. Geology is important, too, as in "Near Bickering," in which the poet notes that the "seam that runs sinewing England / Crops out" in the north so that he recognizes the "colour of home, the Cotswold colour, / Across these high wolds . . . / In the free-stone barrier that divides / Lawn from corn-field." Wherever Tomlinson's eye alights, there is a sense of Gerard Manley Hopkins's "sweet, especial rural scene."

Frankly, I find that I prefer Tomlinson's landscapes when they are peopled. The book opens with a sequence entitled "For a Granddaughter," and examines "the ties of blood / Rooting us in place," much as rhyme links the elements of a poem. Two of the best poems are addressed to other poets and situate them in particular landscapes. "To Vasko Popa in Rome" includes an elegiac portrait of the Yugoslav poet ("the least imperious of men") walking among the "imperial pretensions" of the eternal city:

> Pacing on,
> Complaining of the melancholy great cities breed,
>   As if all generosity must feed that, too,
> You drew your gloom from a reserve of riches
>   That soon must fail. In Rome, today,
> I almost persuade myself you would agree
>   That the bounty of the place exceeds pretension. . . .

One becomes aware of a certain self-criticism in these lines. Tomlinson's weakness is not pretentiousness so much as an inclination to aestheticize. In "To a Yorkshireman in Devon," written for Donald Davie's seventieth birthday, he recalls that Davie once criticized his poetry for "gild[ing] rural scenes inordinately." He also brings up the subject of the Gloucestershire poet and composer Ivor Gurney, who was wounded and gassed in the Great War and later suffered from mental illness. Having to address a poem to Davie, himself austerely intellectual and focused in his poetry, keeps Tomlinson from indulging in rural French:

> I could not live only on leaves and grass
> For all my equanimity, but let that pass.
> Gurney thanked God for Gloucestershire. You see
> At once how a mere county boundary
> Could not explain the intentions of the Lord.

Tomlinson works out a very interesting idea about Gurney's feeling for England. He believes that it was based on a feeling for "land that is worked." In a disquisition on England as Eden, Tomlinson shares his view that Gurney's Eden (and one suspects Tomlinson's, too) "means / The practicality of rural scenes / Besides the poetry of place—divine / And human. . . ."

An autumnal light bathes many of the poems, including the title poem, "Jubilación." A note explains that the word is Spanish and means retirement. Like the poem for Davie this one is in heroic couplets, but it's more of a ramble, talking about how the poet spends his day with his wife, now that he's "free." The poem is subtitled "a letter to Juan Malpartida," and it has an epistolary looseness that makes a reader wonder when the poet is going to get to the point. But there is no point, really, except a renewed awareness of "the great cycle of the ceaseless year."

If I sound lukewarm about this book, I'm afraid I am. There is only one poem in which Tomlinson's temperature rises, and that is "To a Christian Concerning Ivor Gurney." A remarkable protest at the fate of a gifted artist, it begins:

> You will have much to explain to your God on the final day,
> And he, also, will have much to explain to you—
> Why (say) the mind of Gurney, whose preludes I am
>   listening to,
> Should, through so many years, have to waste away
> Into inconsequence—composer, poet who dreamed that our
>   land
> Would greet in him an heir of Jonson and Dowland. . . .

The poem, coming toward the end of the book, is like a flashpoint. It shows a passion that might have given a greater intensity to this collection, if it had caught fire in the other poems.

On this side of the Atlantic, Louis Simpson's collection *There You Are*, his fifteenth by my count, demonstrates once again that no one writing today has a better understanding of narrative as a figure of speech. Each of his stories is like a piece standing for life as a whole, existing in a kind of chaste simplicity and yet, to paraphrase Simpson himself, giving off vibrations. Those vibrations have much to do with Simpson's awareness that, to paraphrase Tip O'Neill on politics, all myth is local myth:

> I give you my friend Roger
> who recently left Denise
> and is living with Diane
> in a motel in Florida.
> Watching daytime television . . .
> Mosquitoes and tractor trailers
> keeping him awake, making his heart race,
> like a clashing of shields
> and swords, and flights of arrows.
>
> *"The Cabin"*

Those vibrations have much to do, as well, with Simpson's wry, even satirical voice. That voice, despite the elemental realism of his current poetry, is one of the richest and most complex of any we have in American writing today. It is in evidence at the end of "Al and Beth," one of the best poems in *There You Are*. After describing his Uncle Al as an impassive man who works in a drugstore near Times Square and his Aunt Beth as an entertainer on cruise ships, Simpson recounts a disagreement with Al about "something that America / was doing." Al's response is "'My country / right or wrong.'" Another poet might have let this character twist on the corkscrew of his cant. But Simpson moves further into character and plot:

> I suppose so, if you've come
> from a village in Russia no one
> ever heard of, with no drains,
> and on saints' days the Cossacks
> descend on you with the blessing
> of the Church, to beat out your brains
> . . . .
>
> Al lived on Kingston Avenue, Brooklyn,
> all of his life, with the wife
> his mother had picked out for him.
> Beth never married. She was still waiting
> for Mr. Right.
>
> > Of such is the Kingdom
> of Heaven. Say that I sent you.

Simpson sends us into the lives of people and their stories. Is there another poet writing in our day who is known for his characters, as Frost and Robinson were known in theirs? In this book there is Mr. Cooper, the physics teacher, "a cross-eyed little Englishman," at the school in Jamaica that Simpson attended as a boy; there are Nipkow and Cosulich, exporters of seconds in New York City; there's Max, "a genius in the family"; there's the reluctant philosopher Joe Butensky who observes, "'Life is like a glass of tea'"; and there are the various associates of Simpson's alter ego Peter in the publishing business—J.J. and Gallagher and Mike, and the second-rate authors they publish. Like Frost and Robinson, Simpson is a poet of the American character and vernacular. Though he spares a character like Uncle Al, he can be unsparing, as well, when he catches a whiff of dishonesty. The first two stanzas of "Honeymoon" are Simpson at his most unforgiving:

> Uncle Bob prayed over the groom:
> "Let him establish Kingdom principles."
> Aunt Shirley prayed for the bride:
> "Father, I pray an anointing on her."
> "Love," said Reverend Philips,
>
> "is insensitive, love is invalueless."
> He said that we merger together
> in holy matrimony,
> and the choir burst into song:
> "He waits for us, and waits for us."

In a poem of some thirty years ago, "In the Suburbs," Simpson complained, "There's no way out." It appears that characters like those in "Honeymoon" are trapped in middle-class lives that make a botch of ceremony and tradition. And yet, that a way out is imaginable, whether through ceremony, tradition, or something else, seems just as American as the failure to escape middle-class vulgarity. Simpson expresses this American dilemma eloquently in the book's last poem, "A Clearing," a memoir of a visit to Australia:

> I stood in the middle of the clearing
> looking at the sky. It was glittering
> with unknown constellations.
> Everything I had ever known
> seemed to have disappeared.
> And who was I, standing there
> in the middle of Australia
> at night? I had ceased to exist.
> There was only whatever it was
> that was looking at the sky
> and listening to the wind.

He retains that clearing as "a place in my mind" where "nothing . . . stands between me / and it, whatever it is." A news story during the 1996 presidential campaign reported that adding the word "whatever" to phrases was a favorite and worrisome habit of speech of Senator Robert Dole. Here Louis Simpson has rescued the word by investing it with an American sense of the sublime. In a world devalued by the speech of Senator Dole and Reverend Philips, we should be grateful that we have Louis Simpson to redeem our language.

British poets like Herbert Lomas and Charles Tomlinson appear to suffer no anxiety about moving between free and metrical verse. Their books include numerous poems in both modes. Louis Simpson is part of that American generation which, having begun their careers as masters of traditional English verse, turned to mastering—indeed, inventing—a new kind of nonmetrical verse, presumably to capture the unique cadence of American speech. There was a typical all-or-nothing American attitude to this revolt when it took place over thirty years ago. But recently this attitude has begun to soften. Simpson himself includes a version of a poem by Corbière in alternating quatrains of iambic trimeter in his new book, and he has published rhymed and metered versions of poems by Mallarmé. The change in attitude is largely due to a younger generation of American poets who have reapprenticed themselves to the modes of English verse that elders like Simpson rejected and who have shown through their recent mastery what should have been clear all along: a poet can sound just as American in the formal verse of Robert Frost as in the free verse of William Carlos Williams.

This generation of American poets has come to be known as the New Formalists. Twenty-one of them are represented in a beautiful, fine-press, limited-edition volume entitled *Formal Introductions,* edited by Dana Gioia, who speculates in his introduction that the New Formalism "may grow into the movement which leads American poetry into the twenty-first century." Paul Lake's "Introduction to Poetry," typical among the poems included for its easy grace, wit, and formal accuracy, makes that speculation seem entirely possible:

She comes in late, then settles like a sigh
On the first day, returning every week
Promptly at ten, each Monday Wednesday Friday,
To study Shakespeare, Jonson, Donne, and Blake;

Enters the room to an approving murmur,
Straightens her dress, then, brushing back her hair,
Arches her body with the slightest tremor,
And sits, while the room grows breathless, in her chair;

Sits for an hour, while busy sophomores worry
Each turgid line, a Botticellian smile
On her rapt face, who's learned how little study
Love involves; who, walking down the aisle,

Knows in her bones how little poetry
Words breathe, and how—on turning to go home—
All eyes will watch her rise above her "C"
And walk off, like a goddess on the foam.

The New Formalism is a welcome phenomenon that restores pleasures that American poetry has been denying itself for too long.

Journals of the Soul

Recently a woman told me that she had been accused of writing like a man because her poems slam shut at the end. One thinks of W. B. Yeats's belief that a poem is finished when it clicks shut like a box and also of Robert Frost saying, "I think a poem should have doors. I wouldn't leave them open though." Yet Emily Dickinson's poems seem like a series of doors or rooms full of doors slamming shut while others open. It is interesting to think of closure as gender specific, but only until exceptions proliferate and form new generalizations. The six poets under review here, all women, have written poems in their new books that click shut and are open-ended. Still, a developing process of thought underlies each book and makes even the most finished of its poems communicate with others around it. That process of thought, though it is the thought of a woman's mind in a woman's body, is distinctly spiritual in tone and inclined to transcend gender. Each of these books is, more or less, the journal of a soul.

Lynn Hejinian's *The Cell* is actually a journal, a series of dated entries beginning October 6, 1986, and ending January 21, 1989. On the page, each entry has a central column with arms extended to the left margin. The language is always about something, but rarely is that something revealed or, if it is, it is not developed for more than a few lines. The entry dated May 21, 1988, begins like this:

Review of *Cell* by Lynn Hejinian, *Evening Train* by Denise Levertov, *Moon Bridge Crossing* by Tess Gallagher, *Bright Existence* by Brenda Hillman, *A Gilded Lapse of Time* by Gjertrud Schnackenberg, and *Two Trees* by Ellen Bryant Voigt from *The Hudson Review* (summer 1993).

> The wonderful muffledness of the
> > moment of solitude which covers
> > the breasts
> They are both locks and
> > lapses
> Words—
> But the moment is very
> > warm—summer arrives without thinking
> > although thought is intruding

The idea of intrusion turns up now and then throughout the book, but what is intruding is often unspecified. If it is thought, does it include the possibility that an entry might resolve into an individual poem? Later, an entry dated September 11, 1988, begins:

> There is pleasure in producing
> > percussion, measure in intrusion
> I like to let there
> > be intrusion

It may be words themselves are the intrusion she speaks of, bringing with them evidence of thought, only to be intruded upon by other words and thoughts. I would call this associative thinking if it were more imagistic, but Hejinian's own description of noise, including music, as having "a continuous destination" is more apt. Association leads to revelation and insight, and in poetry it may lead to closure. Hejinian's writing is as close to composition by field as anyone has come. A reader can enter the 217 pages of *The Cell* anywhere without feeling lost.

I am not going to pretend I like this kind of thing, because I don't. Yet Hejinian is probably the most talented of the so-called Language Poets and escapes their ideological methods by sheer wit. Her riff on motherhood, in the entry for June 5, 1988, suggests that she can take herself and her methods lightly. Stating that "women and money" are "absolutely necessary to motherhood," she concludes:

And so it is that
        mothers because they purchase so
        much—the greatest amount of
        purchasing is done by mothers
        —do it regularly, anywhere, and
        very often, until it's hardly
        visible, something white behind a
        green medium—spring and a
        cascade of peas!

The open-endedness of the poems may be a response to the confinement of domesticity. The title of her book, *Cell*, with its suggestion of confinement and closure, contrasts with the actual structure of its poems, and yet Hejinian's art is really quite domestic, even homely, without the glamour we sometimes associate with the so-called avant garde. The poetry in *Cell* is more like furniture-moving, arranging things provisionally while at the same time saying, "Read this and tell me what it says." Her poems present a grid and a mind, often a very appealing and felicitous mind:

This is the way I
        want to go in and
        out of heaven—with depth
        perception.

One can imagine Emily Dickinson recognizing this feeling. As with all such writing, I keep reading to understand until I understand that understanding may not be the reason for reading. Yet what I perceive as the soul of Hejinian's poetry is not ultimately formless, though I cannot describe it.

Denise Levertov's *Evening Train* forms a long sequence about growing older, with a terrific payoff. This is the best writing she has done in years. Her strengths have always been a superb ear and a gift for the free verse line. These are present from the book's beginning, in the first section entitled "Lake Mountain Moon." Here is all of "Presence":

Though the mountain's the same warm-tinted ivory
as the clouds (as if a red ground had been laid beneath
not quite translucent white) and though the clouds
disguise its shoulders, and rise tall to the left and right,
and soften the pale summit with mist,
                                        yet one perceives
the massive presence, obdurate, unconcerned
among those filmy guardians.

As she searches for meaning among her subjects, she expresses
its discovery without coyness or archness. Whether she is imag-
ining Ruskin in Yosemite or the similarity between migrating
salmon and memory, she is excellent company. Even as she
dwells on her own aging, she brings to it her finest lyric gifts, as
in these lines from "Broken Pact":

A face ages quicker than a mind.

And thighs, arms, breasts,
take on an air of indifference.
Heart's desire has wearied them, they chose to forget
whatever they once promised.

But mind and heart continue
their eager conversation. . . .

Levertov is especially good in the book's longer poems, like
"Letter to a Friend," "Link," and "Dream Instruction." In the
last she addresses an "old mother sitting in bed" who becomes
an image of someone who has "come to live in what happens,
not in the telling." In the title poem, the poet watches an old
man sleeping in her train compartment, then realizes:

I called him old, but then I remember
my own age, and acknowledge he's likely
no older than I. But in the dimension
that moves with us but in itself keeps still
like the bubble in a carpenter's level,
I'm fourteen, watching the faces I saw each day
on the train going in to London
and never spoke to; or guessing
from a row of shoes what sort of faces
I'd see if I raised my eyes.

When Levertov is writing like this, she is the equal of any poet we have today.

A weakness of the book reflects a weakness and strength of Levertov's career: the desire to be topical. During the Vietnam War, Levertov wrote some of the best poems against the conflict along with some of the worst. *Evening Train* includes poems about a gay man's estrangement from his parents, wife-beating, and the Gulf War. None of them is very good, but some include lines whose exactness and music transcend the political intent that motivated them, like these from "In California During the Gulf War":

> Among the blight-killed eucalypts, among
> trees and bushes rusted by Christmas frosts,
> the yards and hillsides exhausted by five years of drought,
>
> certain airy white blossoms punctually
> reappeared. . . .

You can hear the drought in those words, in the inner rhyming of "rusted," "frosts," and "exhausted," offset by the extraordinary line about blossoms and the inspired word "punctually."

When she turns from the topical, as if leaving behind a list of completed assignments, Levertov comes back to her ongoing meditation on aging. The second to last poem, "The Tide," is the kind of poem that could be written only by someone who had paid close attention to experience as she grew older. These lines provide a metaphor you could almost live by:

> Clean the littered beach, clear
> the lines of a forming poem,
> the waters flood inward.
> Dull stones again fulfill
> their glowing destinies, and emptiness
> is a cup, and holds
> the ocean.

Tess Gallagher's *Moon Bridge Crossing* is the journal of a soul trying to deal with an irrevocable loss. It contains sixty poems, and the best of them concern the death of her husband. Whenever his presence is felt, it focuses the poet, gives her the discipline of some inherent form (even if it is only the address) to keep her from her tendency to create diffuse or clotted passages of writing that seem to be no more than poeticizing. The book's first poem is one of its most successful. It is uncharacteristically brief, austere, and lucid. Here it is in full, the poem "Yes":

> Now we are like that flat cone of sand
> in the garden of the Silver Pavilion in Kyoto
> designed to appear only in moonlight.
>
> Do you want me to mourn?
> Do you want me to wear black?
>
> Or like moonlight on whitest sand
> to use your dark, to gleam, to shimmer?
>
> I gleam. I mourn.

She enacts a number of private rituals in the ghostly presence of her husband and some with his corpse. In "Paradise" she explains how a friend who "had been staying awake for me" leaves her alone with her husband's body. She describes speaking to him and rubbing his feet with oil. But the final stanza grows increasingly hermetic, pulling further away from the moving clarity of her moment with her dead husband. It appears to be offered as insight:

> For to confirm what is forever beyond speech
> pulls actions out of us. And if it is only childlike and
> unreceived, the way a child hums to the stick
> it is using to scratch houses into the dirt, still
> it is a silky membrane and shining
> even to the closed eye.

I am with her until the final two lines. She often compares her own actions to those of a child or depicts herself as a girl. But just as often she employs pretty, ornamental, and finally obscure images like the "silky membrane" bit here.

The obscure and ornamental so predominate the book that when she comes to the book's other truly fine poem, "I Stop

Writing the Poem," I ask myself why she does not stop more often.

I Stop Writing the Poem

to fold clothes. No matter who lives
or who dies, I'm still a woman.
I'll always have plenty to do.
I bring the arms of his shirt
together. Nothing can stop
our tenderness. I'll get back
to the poem. I'll get back to being
a woman. But for now
there's a shirt, a giant shirt
in my hands, and somewhere a small girl
standing next to her mother
watching to see how it's done.

Other themes, even techniques, even phrases from Gallagher's previous work are echoed here, like the use of the title as a first line, the function of domestic chores as a way of dealing with grief, and the persona of the girl. But on the facing page, in "Cherry Blossoms," she remembers a dog who befriended her in childhood this way:

Miles of night and her wild vowellings under
great moons, subsiding into a kind of atrocious
laughter, what I think of now as faint gleams
of demoniac nature ratifying itself.

This language is simply overwrought. Gallagher has always been best in the short, spare, basically narrative lyric, and that is how she is best in this book of grief.

Tess Gallagher has a powerful emotion at heart, and that may be what leads her to excess. Gjertrud Schnackenberg does not appear to have anything at heart but the desire to dazzle. *A Gilded Lapse of Time* abounds with references to gold, glittering, and gilt. Though many of the references have to do with the decay of Western art, the failures to preserve myth, the expense of spirit in a waste of paint, and finally the suffering of the artist (her long last section is about Osip Mandelstam), the end result is superficial glamour. Fool's gold.

Of course, Schnackenberg is not a fool. Her previous book, *The Lamplit Answer,* showed her to be capable of wit and cunning self-analysis rendered with an elegant sense of style. It could be that confronting the shades of Dante, Piero della Francesca, and Osip Mandelstam is all too much for her, despite the voluminous notes at the end of her book that attest to her erudition. It certainly sets my teeth on edge to hear her patronize each of these great artists with direct addresses ("Dante, in paradise, as you climbed, / From the starry paths you must have seen / The mansions that stood uninhabited // In empty Florence"), but there is also something puzzling about the book's entire project, especially when considering who is writing it. Most of the poems are written in slack pentameter or trimeter lines, but without any of Schnackenberg's typical use of rhyme. The only formal principle seems to be to keep sentences running as long as possible, extending them with the aid of conjunctions until it becomes not so much a relief that a sentence ends, but a surprise. Nor is there any sense that she is making her way toward enlightenment or epiphany, as she so remarkably achieved in the title poem of *The Lamplit Answer.* The poems here aren't strings—that would be too modest a metaphor—but chains of details, as if she were following the fossilized spines of dinosaurs vertebra after vertebra into rock. Only when she enters the third and final part of her book does she achieve something like emotive power, largely due to what we know of Mandelstam's tragedy. Yet there is something heartless in her imagining an ideal world for him, as in these lines:

> You will be free to wander
> In the metropolitan library,
> Free to stare,
> Without arousing suspicion,
> At the statue voted by the senate
> To honor Poetry,
> Once a block of undifferentiated marble
> Originally destined, in the old life,
> For a grandiloquent hotel lobby
> In the Empire style. . . .

What makes *A Gilded Lapse of Time* seem like the journal of a soul is the final and most successful poem, which identifies the speaker as part of a misanthropic tradition that includes D. H. Lawrence. Having surveyed Western history through its most powerful myth—Christianity—and its deadliest metaphor—totalitarianism—Schnackenberg ends by writing:

> If I could begin again,
> Time is something I would measure
> In generations of roses, evolving across
> Gulfs we have no records of,
> Eons without witnesses,
> Without surviving portraits. . . .

The poem extends its conceit for seven pages in which Schnackenberg effectively does away with history, but the surfeit chokes the reader. It is a tour de force, but that is all it is.

Robert Frost maintained that poetry's height is "the philosophical attempt to say matter in terms of spirit, or spirit in terms of matter, to make the final unity." Though he also added that this attempt inevitably fails or stops short, still he thought it the "greatest of all attempts to say one thing in terms of another." I believe that is what Brenda Hillman has done in *Bright Existence*—tried to find that mediating metaphor between body and soul that not only establishes a similitude but expresses the absolute identity of each.

Where Gjertrud Schnackenberg might seek a revelation in the Uffizi, Brenda Hillman has hers in Baskin Robbins. "Old Ice" is representative of the many commonplace situations in which Hillman engages in uncommon meditation:

> You stood in the ice cream shop
> and from the street, in a group
> of silly glass trumpets
> light came,
> and broke into millions of itself, shattered
> from the pressure of being mute who knows how long.

In the book's first poem, "Little Furnace," a voice tells the poet that she is not only the shape but the meaning of her life. "Old

Ice" ends with a reflection on poetry's former role and a projection into the book's concerns, as stated in "Little Furnace":

> Once it seemed the function of poetry
> was to redeem our lives.
> But it was not. It was to become
> indistinguishable from them.

Brenda Hillman's imagistic gift is great, the strongest feature of her previous books, *Fortress* and *White Dress,* but like Frost she also has a gift for phrasing, for catching the tones of a speaker's thought. We can hear it in "First Thought." Describing the birth of her daughter, she writes, "The first thought / was rage."

> The moment my daughter was lifted
> from me, that sticky
> flesh screamed fury,
> for she, too, blamed the female body—
> I loved it that she screamed—
>
> and I knew I had been sent to earth to understand that pain.

Gnosticism is behind much of the book's impulse, and if we recoil from that mode of thinking, which negates the equation between matter and spirit, then we ought to look more closely at what Hillman's words say, rather than what a few of her epigraphs suggest. "First Thought" ends on a note rooted in Frost's understanding of Jamesian pragmatism:

> The last pain on earth will not be the central pain,
> it will be the pain of the soul and not the body,
> the pain of the body will be long since gone,
> absorbed into the earth, which made it beautiful—
>
> don't you love the word raiment?
> Dawn comes in white raiment.
> Something like that.

It takes a peculiarly American sense of the ineffable to write a phrase like "Something like that." It was in such pronouns—*something, that*—that Frost and Stevens conveyed the sublimity they could not or would not otherwise name. So does Brenda Hillman, at her best.

I do have an objection to the approach of some of the poems here, because of added quirks to a style that is sufficient without them. Hillman has attempted to assimilate some of the strategies of the Language Poets. Thus she will play with punctuation, lining up excess commas or ending poems with a dash, and interrupt the sequence of the book with breathless, parenthetical passages, each called "(interruption)." One of these "(interruption)"'s, coming after a poem about the good life in Berkeley, entitled "Several Errands," shows a flash of cheerful sarcasm:

> (—a man told me I better think
> about my "system."
> Oh dear! I better
> think about my "system"—!)

But others appear to be more invested in their absences and erasures, in their failure to mean than in their meaning.

> (—Faster messed up poor only
> helper go
> faster, and the soul said sorry
> my this one I can't go any faster—)

> (—then I asked how
> far should I go.
> Go deeper, the voice said;
> it was double—)

What was "double"? The voice? The distance? Or does "double" modify something unstated, existing on the other side of the dash? If Hillman were to think about her "system," she would know that she does not need that kind of mannerism.

The poem "A Foghorn," which follows a particularly self-conscious experiment called "untitled fragments," is proof that Hillman's imagination is greater than the artifice of Language Poetry. Imagining "all the divorced Californians" come out to the beach to watch the gray whale migration, she writes with profound humanity:

They wait as if at the prow of a fatherless ship,
leaning there; they have waited a long time,
they are so used to waiting, they have waited for
the winning number, or for the changes in someone,
or for the nocturne to rewind itself around the spool—
shouldn't something have pity on them now?

One name for that something is poetry, like the poetry in *Bright Existence*. It is a wonderful book.

So, too, is Ellen Bryant Voigt's *Two Trees*. It is, however, more restrained than Brenda Hillman's, less in search of the meaning of experience and less given to generalization, to the epigrammatic summary that is what we often bring away from a poem. It is more concerned with the contours, the drama, of events. Classical material, both in myth and music, defines many of the poems. The book begins with how the artist or anyone for that matter makes her way toward articulation, toward that expression that creates the self. The most difficult, but the most beautiful poem is the first one, "First Song," which meditates on the figure of Hermes:

> Shepherd, Augur
> Patron of Thieves, who had once been
> Master of Invention
> . . . .
> who gave the world the musical scale,
> sounds become a sweetness and a power;
> who gave the world the alphabet,
> the mind made supple as the hand;
> who gave the world hymns of invocation,
> seven vowels uttered in succession,
> so mortals might petition
> blind fortune. . . .

"First Song" is followed by "Effort at Speech," a homage to William Meredith and his poem of the same title and indirectly, I imagine, to Muriel Rukeyser, to whom Meredith dedicated his poem and who also wrote a poem called "Effort at Speech." Voigt's records an encounter with an even stranger otherness than their poems do. Through the glass wall of an aquarium, she watches a ray, "huge, delta-winged, bat-winged, / head subsumed in the spread pectorals." The final lines of the poem echo two other poems about the mind's attempt to articulate itself—Richard Wilbur's "Mind" and Theodore Roethke's "Night Crow":

> it skated along the glass—
> eagle scanning the sheer canyon wall,
> bat trapped inside the cave,
> no, like a mind at work, at play,
> I felt I was seeing through the skull—
> and then away.

This poem, so unlike "First Song," is followed by "At the Piano," which is unlike "Effort at Speech." Yet together the three form a chord that resonates throughout the book. It is the music of self-knowledge. Here are the opening lines of "At the Piano":

> At the piano, the girl, as if rowing upstream,
> is driving the triplets against the duple meter,
> one hand for repetition,
> one hand for variation and for song.
> She knows nothing, but Bach knows everything.
> Outside, in the vast disordered world,
> the calves have been taken from their mothers;
> both groups bawled and hooted all night long—
> she heard them from her quilted double bed.

This persona, represented in some of Voigt's finest poems, is the daughter of a farmer, and the poignancy of her life is the potential split between the demands of art and family. The poem ends, "she knows nothing, she thinks / no one could be happier than this."

Knowledge, the acquisition of knowledge, and the inevitable cost concern Voigt throughout *Two Trees*. Its title poem retells the story of how the appetite for knowledge was acquired. Once expelled from the garden, "the mind cried out / for that addictive tree it had tasted." The other tree, the second tree, is of course the tree of eternal life; its fruit if tasted would have made us invulnerable to suffering. The final poem of *Two Trees* shows us Voigt's persona, herself now a grown woman and a mother, watching another girl, perhaps a daughter, "strapped in the bare mechanical crib" in a hospital. The drama of knowledge without the ability to end suffering is powerfully enacted.

Three of the poems in *Two Trees* come with sets of variations. Untitled, each of these ranges from the lyric to the aphoristic but suggests that there is something more to be gotten out, to be expressed. My favorite is only two lines long:

> —Have you always told the truth?
>
> I have always loved the truth.

That is the best answer, I think, any of us can give.

Body and Soul
Parts of a Life

Nora

My maternal grandmother, Nora Pemberton, was a dedicated reader and writer. She loved Emily Dickinson, Dorothy Parker, and Samuel Pepys. She grew up with four brothers and a sister in Wiggins, Mississippi, where her father, Alonso Bodie, worked for the lumber industry. I have been told that her mother was a quarter Choctaw. The Native American features showed more in her sister's face than in Nora's, but the pictures I have seen of my great-grandmother, Allie Bodie, are striking. She had straight black hair and high cheekbones. Alonso Bodie's parents were from County Cork. Because he was not satisfied to be the engineer of a small lumber train, he would tell strangers he drove for the B & O Line.

Nora was not satisfied with her life, either. She divorced my mother's father, James Foster, when my mother was only four years old and later married Elmer Pemberton. After World War II, when Granddaddy Pemberton, who liked to be called Pup Dog, got out of the Navy, he started Dependable Maintenance, a caretaking and salvage company, in San Diego. His place of business, as Nora called it, was located on Newton Avenue. It included a bar known as the Total Loss Room where Pup Dog spent a lot of his free time. Nora sat at home writing stories and poems, chewing Pepsin Gum, and smoking Chesterfields, or she took Yellow Cabs around San Diego. She suffered from a mild form of epilepsy, but also had nervous breakdowns periodically.

From *Contemporary Authors, Autobiography Series* (Detroit: Gale Research, Inc., 1996).

Her epileptic seizures resulted in temporary memory loss. When she took her parakeet for walks around the neighborhood, attached to her wrist by a strand of yarn, it was usually a sign of a nervous breakdown. She had a fondness for horse racing. After she died at the age of fifty-nine, of a botched surgery for a blocked bowel, Pup Dog claimed that she had squandered a fortune gambling at Del Mar, the track north of San Diego.

When I visited them as a child, Pup Dog would take me to the place of business, and I would be free to roam his warehouse, reading magazines or racy paperbacks from fire and flood losses while he worked or drank in the Total Loss Room. He had a collection of military rifles of all vintages, Japanese, German, and American. Once after work he set up a bucket of sand at one end of the warehouse and let me fire an M-1 rifle clip into it. I must have been eleven at the time. Usually I stayed home with Nora and played with a group of boys on her street who all called her by her first name. When she wrote, either she typed at her kitchen table or lounged on her recliner beside an enormous *Webster's* and revised typescript. She was thin as a slat. She would tell me, referring to the dictionary on its stand, that she lived in that book, and I could see her slipping easily between the pages. Toward the end of her life (I was twelve when she died) she acquired a dictaphone and would record her writing on belts of wide red tape. She wrote a story called "A Giant in the House" about an uncle living with his young niece and nephew, a poem about a lizard who was a dandy and made his money as a landlord, and she tried to publish a cookbook for husbands, *Serve While Hot*, "dedicated to men who like to play around in the kitchen." It was interspersed with jokes and poems, like the following that headed the chapter "Baked Goose":

> The goose appears to be
> As cheerful as a clown.
> But he is only bluffing
> For underneath he's down.

I have the manuscripts of some of her stories and poems, and I also have the dictaphone belts. After Nora died, Pup Dog moved the dictaphone machine that she used to his place of business. Shortly before he died himself, Dependable Maintenance burned to the ground and, I believe, other manuscripts of Nora's which were stored there were also lost.

She published little during her life, but when she did she preferred to use the pen name Louise Verne. My parents regarded her as an oddity, and I never knew until much later, when I started to write, how much I owed her. In her presence, I must have learned that writing was something people did, people you knew, your own family members. I know I also learned the romance of embellishment, fabrication, and lying. She was proud, for example, of the fact that Pup Dog, who had little schooling, was even more widely read than she. Supposedly he had read Gibbon's *Decline and Fall of the Roman Empire* before he was a teenager. Once I got into an argument with a boy in her neighborhood, one of my playmates when I visited San Diego, about the fall of Rome. My friend had a seen a movie in which it appeared that Rome fell in a day. I was certain that it had taken years, if not centuries. We asked Nora to settle our argument (I don't know why we didn't ask Pup Dog), and she took my side, informing my friend that, after all, *I* had read Gibbon's *Decline and Fall of the Roman Empire*. It was an impressive tactic. For awhile I even believed her myself.

For many years I had the idea of writing a series of poems based on her dictaphone belts. My poem "Writing for Nora," included in my first book, *North Sea,* refers to them as "lost." Though I found them later, I could never locate the right kind of machine to play them. In 1987 when I began drafting my book-length, narrative poem *Iris,* which is based in part on Nora's life, I tried to give my character some of Nora's same interests as a reader, especially her passion for the diaries of Samuel Pepys. She loved his account of the Great Fire of London, and at bedtime she would announce, "And so to bed." But reading the diaries myself, as I began to create Iris, I found it impossible to get excited about Pepys or imagine Iris, a college dropout from Western Kentucky, reading him with Nora's enthusiasm. Instead I gave Iris an obsession with the poet Robinson Jeffers, no less outlandish, I admit, but an interest that coincided with my own.

Ray

I am the son and grandson of preachers. My father, Donald Ray Jarman, was ordained into the Christian Church (Disciples of Christ) in 1950, just after he graduated from Chapman College, which at that time was still located in Los Angeles, California. His father, Ray Jarman, was ordained into the same denomination in 1912, in Kansas City, Missouri, when he was seventeen years old.

Ray Jarman's first pastorate was a little church in the mining town of Bevier, Missouri. He said that people came from miles around to hear the boy preacher and that when he left, the congregation had grown by 500 percent. Throughout his life, wherever he preached, he counted on the enthusiastic receptions of large crowds. As a young man he also traveled from church to church, as a kind of circuit rider. One night he had to share a hotel room and a bed with a man who returned late in the evening, wearing a gun.

Ray claimed that his mother's mother and Samuel Clemens's mother were sisters. Though the actual relationship is much more distant, it provoked Ray's lifelong interest in Mark Twain (my namesake). He made himself something of an expert on Twain's life and work, and in the days before Twain imitators, he would earn extra money lecturing on Twain, telling anecdotes based on the writer's life, reciting passages from his letters, and retelling his stories.

My grandfather had a phenomenal memory, one he had trained with a simple mnemonic technique that was taught to me by my father. He memorized by pacing back and forth, tracing and retracing his steps in a hall or in the backyard, sometimes extending his range and reversing direction, while adding passages as he established a physical rhythm. In this way he had memorized much of the New Testament. On Sunday when it was time to read the Scripture lesson, he impressed his congregation by saying the verses with the Bible closed. When I was a child I thought he knew the entire Bible by heart. Along with Twain and the Bible, he liked to quote Kipling's poem "When Earth's Last Picture Is Painted," and Emily Bronte's "Last Lines," which begins "No coward soul is mine." One of his favorite passages, which I heard him recite numerous times even after he became a charismatic Christian evangelist, was Marie Corelli's description of the Crucifixion in her novel *Barabbas*.

After serving churches in the Midwest, Ray took his family in the early 1940s to Los Angeles, where he was pastor of Huntington Park Christian Church. Ray had always had a fascination with what he called the transcendent or the metaphysical, which was often simply the supernatural or unconventional. In the pulpit he claimed that he heard the voice of his dead mother speaking to him. In the balmy, palmy climate of Southern California, when towns like Huntington Park were still surrounded by orange groves and dairy farms, Ray discovered all kinds of unconventional spirituality. He built a church in South Gate and began a ministry that included a heady range of what today might be called New Age theologies. He preached about the power of positive thinking, yoga, diet, clairvoyance, and dream analysis both from the pulpit and on his radio show, "The Shepherd of the Air." For a brief time he hired lecture halls around Los Angeles and gave talks about conquering the aging process with the help of a youthful-looking elderly man who claimed to be so old he could not reveal his age. Finally, in the early 1960s, he took part in experiments with LSD.

Ray's experiences with the drug were religious and gave him something he had sought, a stronger, fuller sense of a spiritual life. His preaching was always passionate and able to overwhelm grown men with emotion. One man was persuaded to try the drug, had a bad trip, and sued Ray and the church. The consequences were disastrous. His church was in an uproar. His wife, my Grandmother Grace, who had suffered since childhood from a heart ailment, grew ill and died. When Jesus Christ came to him in his office and asked why he had turned away from the Gospel, Ray was born again. He lost his church—for them, his Damascus experience was the last straw—and spent the next fifteen years, almost until his death in 1980, witnessing to his redemption from modernist theology and the drug world.

Ray was an influential presence in my growing up, not so much because of his direct relationship with me, but because of his relationship with my father. During the years when he went farther and farther out, he and my father quarreled bitterly over the church and the nature of faith. After he was born again, his new embrace of the Gospel, which my father had never let go, could make him insufferably righteous. Toward the end of his life, he was living in a home for senior citizens run by Aimee Semple McPherson's Four Square Gospel Church, that quintessential creation of California balminess. There he came to loathe the pious superiority of his fellow inmates. Debilitated by strokes, aware of how he had alienated his son, he managed a partial reconciliation with my father. Yet when he died the same day as Groucho Marx and Mae West, my father took a grim satisfaction in knowing that the crowds greeting them in the next world would be larger than Ray's.

Ray's life and the conflict between him and my father have been the subjects of many of my poems. They form strands that begin in *North Sea* with the poems "History," "Altar Calls," and "Father, Son, and Ghost," and run through my second book, *The Rote Walker,* which takes its title from Ray's technique of memorizing while walking and tries to examine in poems like "1912" and "To Make Flesh" just what it meant to have both Ray's spiritual hunger and, as my father would say, his greed for recognition. In *The Black Riviera,* my fourth book, I tried to capture Ray's response to his wife's illness in the poem "The Death of God."

Scotland

In 1958 when I was six years old, my family moved to Kirkcaldy, Scotland, a linoleum factory town in Fife, on the Firth of Forth, across from Edinburgh. My father had been serving a church in Santa Maria, California, and that spring he had heard of a program called Fraternal Aid to British Churches. Our denomination was sending young ministers and their families for three-year stints to Great Britain to help keep alive its flagging brother churches. At the time, my father's church in Santa Maria was completing a large new sanctuary. Vandenburgh Air Force Base nearby was expanding, and the word was that the whole area would enjoy a new prosperity as a result, with many new members for Santa Maria's churches. My father had just turned thirty. He expressed his interest in going abroad to the church's head office in Indianapolis. On September 17, he, my mother, my four-year-old sister Katie, and I were aboard the *Empress of Britain,* a Canadian Pacific ocean liner, embarked from Montreal to Greenock.

We lived for three years in a semidetached bungalow, the church's parsonage or manse, at 19 Bennochy Road, across from the town's cemetery and in the shadow of one of the Nairn's Linoleum factories. Kirkcaldy, with about fifty thousand people, was known as the Lang Toon, for the way it was strung out along the Firth of Forth. It was said to have been built on the Devil. On mornings when the reek of linseed from the factories was especially strong, droll Kirkcaldians asked, "Can ye no smell 'im?"

The Church of Scotland was Presbyterian, of course, and the Christian Church (Disciples of Christ) was a small presence. My father served St. Clair Street Church of Christ, a very modest, very plain, gray sandstone building on one of Kirkcaldy's busiest streets. The congregation could not have numbered more than one hundred, but during the three years my father served the church, young people were more actively involved than ever before or since. The church elders would hear an innovative suggestion from my father and respond, "We dinnae do it that way." And yet he must have persuaded them to do a number of things "that way," at least for that time. Nearly twenty years later when I returned to Scotland for the first time, I attended a Palm Sunday service at St. Clair Street Church of Christ. The turnout was sparse and made up mostly of older people who had been the older people when I was a boy. I asked one member who had been a teenager when we lived in Scotland what had happened. He said simply, "Your father left."

Kirkcaldy was a dour place, but I only discovered that when I returned years later. It had a castle, Ravenscraig, a black, dangerous ruin on a sea cliff at the east end of town. On the town's west end, Michael Beveridge, a nineteenth-century linoleum magnate, had endowed a park. In the fall, just after school started, there was an evening festival in Beveridge Park. Lights and ornaments were strung through the chestnut trees, and the story of the Babes in the Woods was represented by illuminated figures that appeared beside the paths. Halfway between my house and Beveridge Park was Abbotshall Church, where Pet Marjorie Fleming was buried. She was a friend of Sir Walter Scott and died before she was nine years old. A statue of her sat atop her grave. She wrote pious meditations, but also witty poems, one of which included the lines, "But she was more than usual calm, / She did not give a single dam." The inscription on her stone read, "The Youngest Immortal in the World of Letters." Down by the water was a long promenade where the wind blew constantly. It had been built to attract tourists. Once trees had been planted along it to create a bosky boulevard, but the wind uprooted them. Every April at the west end of the promenade the Links Market took place as it had since the twelfth century. The modern attractions included dodg'em cars, a haunted house, and tents for adults only. Best of all was the helter skelter, a dark wooden tower girdled with a spiral slide. You climbed up on the inside and stepped out at the top for the ride down on a rush mat. Not only could you see everything below, but if the day was fair you could look across the Firth of Forth to Edinburgh and the green saddle of Arthur's Seat with Edinburgh Castle and the Scott Monument set near it like black chess pieces.

Our house was heated by coal-burning fireplaces. The one in the livingroom heated the water. Instead of a refrigerator there was a granite slab in the kitchen pantry that kept things like milk and meat fresh for a couple of days. It seemed almost impossible to get laundry completely dry. In the morning before I went to school my mother would hang my damp kneesocks (I wore short pants) on a small paraffin stove someone had given us, and if we weren't careful, the elastic around their tops would crisp like bacon. The night we arrived, the house was full of people from church who were there to greet us. My sister and I were put to bed by a woman who told us quite cheerfully before she put out the light that every house in Scotland had a ghost. The ghost in that house was the cold. One winter night it split the wooden toilet seat in the bathroom with a sound like a gunshot.

My father took up gardening in Kirkcaldy in order to have something to talk about with the church elders, who all gardened as a hobby. He grew roses and favored those with names like

Forty-Niner, Texas Centennial, and Newport News. My mother kept house, shopping from the vendors who stopped by—the vegetable man with his horsecart and the fishman in a sea-green van—or walking into town with an enormous purse and a floral pocketbook, standard shopping equipment. At first she dazzled people, especially the wee wifeys in the church, with her bright California clothes, but traded them eventually for more subdued attire. Within a year my parents were both ready to return to the United States.

But living in Scotland gave them an opportunity to travel. We toured the Highlands, visited the Netherlands and Belgium, and during the summer of 1961 before we returned to the States, we traveled by car through France, Italy, Switzerland, Germany, Austria, and the principality of Liechtenstein. My parents loved Italy, and my clearest memories are of our weeks there. In Milan we saw Leonardo's "Last Supper," and my father bought a copy painted on silk that he later framed and hung in his office at church. We saw the bones of ancient Christians in the catacombs outside of Rome, and Pope John XXIII blessed us in a huge crowd at St. Peter's.

My parents took a distinct dislike to their fellow American tourists, especially those who complained about the lack of American amenities. Yet when we visited Pisa, they decided we should spend the night in an American-style motel called the California Hotel. The name alone worked on their homesickness (we had been gone from the United States for three years). There were no rooms to accommodate the four of us, so we took two, with my father and me in one and my mother and sister in the other. That night we ate at a restaurant near the hotel. My parents drank Chianti and ate a baked dish made of green pasta. They seemed very happy, and my sister and I were at an age when their happiness made us happy. We walked back to our rooms in a gay mood as a small black thundercloud, with brilliant horns of cartoon lightning, trolled toward us from the horizon. It was hot and muggy, and we opened the louvered windows in our rooms. There were window screens in my mother and sister's room, but none in my father's and mine. Before dawn, my father and I were awakened by the downpour and the sound of thousands of mosquitoes that had taken refuge in our bedroom. A plump little boy, I was a mosquito feast. And for days after in our travels when people regarded my purple, pox-like mosquito bites, my parents would say, "Pisa. Mosquitoes." They also reproached themselves for having chosen a hotel because its name appealed to their nostalgia.

Later, in Vaduz, Liechtenstein, my father became ill from a meal of cannelloni. The woman doctor who examined him scoffed and said it was indigestion. His meal had not agreed with him, she said, probably because he was "a foreigner."

The experience of foreignness lingers from those years abroad. I learned to read in Scotland, sounding vowels out according to the instructions of my first teacher, Miss Reid, a large woman with wild white hair. She banished my American accent. Both my sister and I did not become bilingual exactly, but we spoke the Fife dialect at school and with our friends. My sister remembers the day she lost her Scottish after we returned to America. In answer to a question, she said, "Yeah, Mom" instead of "Aye, Mither."

We adapted ourselves to holidays, too, but it was hard at first. Our first Halloween my sister and I dressed up and went from door to door, saying "Trick or treat!" We were greeted by puzzlement. One woman gave us an orange, another a sixpence. Then a gang of boys came to our house towing a strawman in a wagon and demanded, "A penny for the Guy!" They were collecting money to buy fireworks for Guy Fawkes Day on November 5. And to this day, when I think of past Christmases, the leaner, more somber figure of Father Christmas stands like a shadow beside Santa Claus.

Our second year in Scotland, around Easter time, I was walking to my piano lesson after school, behind a teacher whose son was in my class and who was walking with his mother. A group of older kids suddenly surrounded me and began shouting about something I did not understand. They wanted to know if I wrote to my aunties and uncles and grannies and granddads in America. If I did, I should tell them to take back their Skybolts. They pursued me for a block or two, taunting me about the mysterious Skybolt, then left off. I was in tears and mystified that the teacher and her son, who were only a few steps ahead of me, had never turned around. Sobbing, I told my piano teacher,

Miss Joy Clark, about what had happened and asked her what it all meant. Obviously she read the papers and knew about the pressure America was putting on Britain to buy their new nuclear missile, the Skybolt. Joy Clark was a cheerful woman whose crooked back made her stand not much taller than I. She comforted me and said that it was not my fault, but she also advised me to ask my parents about it. She told me that America could be a very demanding friend.

North Sea takes its title from those years in Scotland and includes a number of poems about my childhood there. The North Sea itself, which in my mind is a chilly gray expanse with long wavering whitecaps like strings drawn across it, mirrors but does not reflect California's Pacific Ocean, the other body of water that appears in my poetry.

I have returned to Kirkcaldy a number of times. The chimneys of the linoleum factories and the factories themselves are gone, moved outside of town or closed completely, due to the lack of demand. The Christian Church (Disciples of Christ) no longer exists in the United Kingdom but has joined the United Reform Church. St. Clair Street Church of Christ, along with an entire parade of shops on its side of the street, was condemned in 1989 so that the street could be widened. Over the years when I visited I would stop by 19 Bennochy Road and see that roses of fairly advanced age, possibly my father's, were still flourishing where he had planted them. And yet the last time I was there, in 1992, his garden had been bricked over to make a patio. The house had become a bed and breakfast. I considered staying there one night, but thought better of it.

Redondo Beach

In 1961, when we returned to the United States, we moved to Redondo Beach, California. When my parents were growing up in Huntington Park, in South Central L.A., they considered Redondo Beach the sticks, an outlying, semiprimitive place. Redondo had a glamorous past as a tourist resort on the south end of Santa Monica Bay. There had been a pavilion, a boardwalk, and a roller coaster, but these were long gone before my parents' time. Once in an old drugstore near the Redondo Pier I found a postcard advertising the city's charms. Redondo had been photographed from the air in black and white, and color tints had been added. It was an enclave, bounded on one side by the nearly purple Pacific and on three others by dense, green-black orange groves. This was the Redondo Beach my parents had known.

In 1961 Redondo was one of a string of slightly seedy beach-towns south of tony Santa Monica. Today, of course, the entire Santa Monica Bay is prime property and the population has been homogenized by upward mobility. My father took the pulpit at South Bay Christian Church. My sister Luanne, who had been conceived in Scotland, was born in South Bay General Hospital the same year. We lived at first in the parsonage on Vincent Street a few blocks from church. I could memorize an entire psalm or chapter from the Bible walking to Sunday school from our house. A few years later my parents bought their own house at the end of Knob Hill. It was too far from church to walk but close enough to the beach that I could carry my surfboard there, if I felt ambitious.

Returning to Southern California, and especially Greater Los Angeles, was important to both my parents. My mother's mother and stepfather lived in San Diego; her father and stepmother lived in the San Fernando Valley. My father probably would have preferred not to be so close to his father, but he had agreed with his sister, who lived in Ohio, that he would be the one to live near their mother, whose health was failing. As a result my sisters and I grew up surrounded by grandparents, pampered, spoiled, and fascinated.

Although I was born in Kentucky, while my father was in seminary in Lexington, and my earliest memories are of the fields and eucalyptus windbreaks near our house in Santa Maria, and my three years in Scotland are like an island of childhood, I think of myself as having grown up in Redondo Beach. And even though the contrast between the North Sea and the Pacific is profound, I still have the feeling that I should be living beside one or the other.

By 1961 the freeway system and the bedroom communities that sprang up around it filled in most of the open spaces between central Los Angeles and the beachtowns, like Redondo, Hermosa, and Manhattan Beach. I can remember driving through a dairy farm and an orange grove on the way to Ray and Grace's house, but those did not last much longer. Redondo was protected from the L.A. Basin's smog and heat by a range of coast hills. When we moved to the house on Knob Hill in 1964, on the hill's crest just above us was a Nike missile base, part of our nation's defense against the Soviet Union's long-range nuclear bombers. Looking up from the end of our driveway we could see the finned white noses of the missiles on their launching pads. It could not have been much later that the base was dismantled and the missiles shipped away, made obsolete by ICBMs. Hemmed in by a half-hearted hurricane fence, the abandoned site with its concrete slabs like patios and its pale green stucco bungalow became a secret gathering place. It remained in the same condition for at least a decade. One night in 1971, home from college, a group of high school friends and I took a jug of rosé to the missile base and watched the moon rise over Mount Baldy. On the exceptional day when the smog had blown south to Riverside County, you could see from that hill all the way to downtown Los Angeles and the San Gabriel Mountains beyond. During the Watts riots it gave us a view of the smoke.

Many of the members of my father's church in Redondo were either in the defense industry or associated with it. They worked for companies like Northrop, McDonnell-Douglas, Hughes Aircraft, Garrett Air Research, and STL, Space Technology Laboratories, which became TRW. They were a conservative bunch, and the 1960s polarized them as they did everyone. My father's attempts to integrate his church or at least to have the church participate in family exchanges with inner-city churches drove people away. When he returned to seminary in Claremont to earn his doctorate, he was influenced by the younger students. After he preached the funeral of a boy in the church who had been blown to pieces in action in Vietnam, my father was soon making it clear from the pulpit that he thought the war was wrong. This too alienated a segment of his congregation. When he left South Bay Christian Church and the pulpit, if not the ministry, in 1971, he was battle-scarred and his congregation was decimated.

I watched what was happening in that church and felt a keen partisanship on my father's behalf. Later, living in other parts of the country, I discovered that people actually believed that life in Southern California was indulgent, worry free, sybaritic, and fake. This strikes me now as too stupid to rebut, but it angered me then and does to this day. When I write about living in that privileged place, since it was beautiful and remains so, I feel moved to show the reality of life there, its urgency and validity.

At least a third of the children I grew up with were Hispanic, most of them Chicano. They were bilingual; the rest of us were not. The divisions did not become pronounced or inflamed until we were in high school. My senior year I played center on the varsity football team and hiked the ball to a boy whose grandparents were from Sonora. Even then our team was mixed like the population of the school. Social pressure was applied increasingly by clubs, gangs, peers, and in the classroom. There were teachers at my high school who did not approve of interracial couples and said as much. The irony is obvious. We were living in a state, a county, a town, and many of us on streets, like Juanita or Catalina, with Spanish names. My junior year there were two brawls after post-game dances between Anglos on the football team and Hispanics who were members of car clubs. The bad blood festered. The next year a lunchtime incident in the student parking lot where cars had been vandalized led to a bizarre and terrifying spontaneous separation of students on the campus. Groups of white and brown kids glared at each other until the bell rang to return to classes. On that occasion the eeriness of what had occurred, though it did not lead to violence, eased tensions. But those of us who had been children together were not children or together any more.

Life with its large resonances—racial strife, suffering in war—and its smaller ones—falling in love for the first time, discovering books—did go on in that place under ideal conditions, I must admit. If it wasn't spring, it was summer. The first day of high school I was waiting in line with a friend to be issued my student ID. My hair had been cut short for football, but my friend was still wearing his long. An officious vice-principal (there was a slew of these creatures at our school) told him to get a haircut. It was a spectacular early September day, actually a typical day for where we lived, and my friend still had sand on his neck from his morning surfing. As soon as school was over that afternoon, he would be back in the water. Stunned by the vice-principal's order, he said in a tone approaching outrage, "But it's still summer!"

I surfed, but I was never very good. Yet I remember being in the water with some of the great surfers of that time, like Mike Doyle and Donald Takayama. It was the sport of truancy, if you were still in school. Huckleberry Finn would have surfed. The beachbreak in Redondo was excellent, until the city attempted to extend the sand to accommodate more tourists and dredged up the gently sloping bottom that allowed the Pacific ground swells to send in glassy breakers that peeled left and right most mornings almost until noon. Eventually the waves reclaimed what had been lost. I could never maneuver very well with the nearly ten-foot boards we rode back then, and preferred body surfing to board surfing. To be lifted, then launched down the face of a wave. To dive under a breaker as the tonnage of foam rushed overhead. To bask as the sun burned through the light morning fog and the water shifted and swelled and the next set of waves formed and came to shore. These were year-round pastimes for me and my friends. They are sensations that return to me in dreams.

Situated in a park above the Redondo Pier was the Redondo Public Library. I discovered truant reading there, the books not assigned at school. Though I did have excellent English teachers who pointed me toward poetry, I found a lot of it on my own, making it all the more precious. There were windows at the end of each aisle of shelves, so much of the place was filled with sunshine during the day. I can remember how the sun fell on the cover of James Dickey's *Buckdancer's Choice* when I first took it off the shelf. And I am sure I read Thom Gunn's "From the Wave," with its description of surfing, for the first time there, and realized that I could write about that, too, maybe even better, though it was a long time before I tried.

My third book, *Far and Away*, is mostly about growing up in Redondo Beach. As the title suggests, it also concerns leaving the place behind.

Teachers

I have been lucky in my teachers, and that may be the reason I make my living as one.

In Scotland, at Dunnikier School, after a period of catching up under the instruction of the fearsome Miss Reid, I had the good fortune to be placed in a class taught by a young woman named Rachel Geddie. Miss Geddie liked Yanks, though like Miss Reid she insisted on the Scottish pronunciation of vowels. She was plump with short curly brown hair and wide-set eyes. I could tell that she wasn't pretty (I measured all women's looks by my mother's who, according to my Scottish friends, was "the prettiest mother"), but Miss Geddie had such a spirit of fun and laughter that she seemed beautiful.

She was a musician and played the piano for the school assembly that took place every Friday morning. Singing was as important in our class as history, geography, and Bible study. She taught us Baring-Gould's "Now the Day Is Over." At the end of the day, when we placed our chairs atop our desks so the janitor could sweep, we sang it instead of saying a prayer. Once when the local Church of Scotland pastor was supervising Bible study in the next classroom, Miss Geddie led us in a rousing rendition of "What Shall We Do with the Drunken Sailor?" She taught us Scottish songs, settings of poems by Burns, and also showtunes from American musicals. She loved *Oklahoma!*

And she found me amusing. One morning she turned to me and said, "Mark, you must be very proud today." I didn't know what she meant. She told me about Alan Shepard's space flight. When another student mentioned that the Russians were still first in space, I challenged him. Miss Geddie was shocked to learn that I did not know or hadn't remembered about Yuri Gagarin. She told me that the *Scotsman* was a very good newspaper. I should read it. When I broke my ankle on the playground trying to leap from a flight of steps, she phoned my mother and helped me to the hospital, and waited with me, and told me about the famous leap of Wallace, the Scottish hero, who jumped from the East Lomond Hill to the West Lomond Hill, which was near Kirkcaldy. Wallace was foully murdered by King Edward I of England, but he was a man with strong ankles.

Miss Geddie spoke to me, as she spoke to all of her pupils, with a directness that made me feel grown-up. Before my family left to return to America, she invited us to a party at her house. When I noticed a framed photograph of her wearing a tiara and an evening gown with bare shoulders, for some reason I asked her why she wasn't married. She didn't seem fazed by the question at all but answered, "Not everybody must be married."

One day while my parents were packing to leave she offered to get my sister and me out of the house by taking us on a walk into the country to Chapeltown, about two miles away. It was a grand adventure at first, on a day of good weather, and Miss Geddie sang and told us stories about growing up in Fife, which wasn't as dour as Kirkcaldy, but as we could see, very beautiful in the countryside. My sister and I faded after an hour. We were used to walking, but this seemed excessive. We never reached Chapeltown, and Miss Geddie insisted that we walk back ourselves. Finally she relented when we found a bus stop and let us ride the rest of the way. I have commemorated that day and Miss Geddie in a poem called "Miss Urquhart's Tiara" in *The Black Riviera*.

When I returned to America, at first we wrote to each other. Once she described a boy in her class who reminded her of me and asked me if I would write to him. I did, but never heard back, and eventually I lost touch with her. While visiting Scotland in 1992 I stopped by Dunnikier School and spoke with a secretary who remembered Rachel Geddie. She told me Miss Geddie had played the piano for Kirkcaldy's Gilbert and Sullivan Society. But she had moved north over twenty years before to teach in a one-room school, and no one at Dunnikier had heard from her since.

I began writing as a freshman in high school and received encouragement, more than I ever deserved, from teachers and friends. I was invited to join the high school writing club, and at one of its first meetings the senior English teacher, James Van Wagoner, spoke. He talked mainly about the necessity of learning to write, if one wished to be a writer, and of writing all the time. "Practice, practice, practice," he said. "Chain yourself to your typewriter." When I asked if talent didn't matter, he said it did not, unless you "practice, practice, practice." He made writing sound like virtuoso piano playing. Years later I discovered that Ezra Pound had the same advice for poets.

Mr. Van Wagoner was handsome, with a long face, wavy brown hair going gray, and a deep widow's peak, and often seemed to be laughing to himself about something. Those of us who admired him wanted in on the joke. He had had some talented students. I knew their work from the high school literary magazine. One of them, Lynne "Squeaky" Fromme, went on to national notoriety but not as a writer. Her poems, which she had written for his class, impressed me. The poet Maurya Simon also studied with him. So did the novelist Rachel Hickerson. They were a couple of years ahead of me, part of a group that included would-be writers, reporters for the school paper, and our high school's version of political activists, all of whom seemed very glamorous to me. Mr. Van Wagoner had taught them all, and he was legendary for his knowledge of modern literature. He was also a poet and novelist, it was said, and he had sold screenplays.

He taught from the old Oscar Williams anthologies of modern and American poetry and let his classes wander through them as they wished. He loved the poetry of Thomas Hardy, Dylan Thomas, and Edna St. Vincent Millay and the fiction of Thomas Wolfe, and talked about the writers' lives, emphasizing their dedication as artists. He was also a James Dickey fan. When I showed him my copy of *Naked Poetry,* which I had discovered at the Either/Or Bookstore in Hermosa Beach, he was interested. He let me write papers about Allen Ginsberg and Denise Levertov.

By the time I took his senior English class I was full of bad writing habits and myself. Yet he saw something in the poems I showed him. Perhaps it was only my avidness. Halfway through the year he told me that instead of attending class I could use the hour to write, but I had to show him my work. He became my first serious reader and critic, and that hour was the first time I had to face what it meant to "practice, practice, practice." I wrote in the teacher's lounge, which was always empty at that time, five days a week, for an hour. When I finished a poem I would show it to him. He would point to a line, or part of a line, a single image, and make a check beside it, and advise me to save it, throw away the rest of the poem, and build a new poem with that little part. He would write terse comments in the margins of poems, almost always having to do with clarity. I was not clear, and I strove to be. He encouraged me to imitate difficult metrical forms by Auden. Once when I used the phrase "Ha, ha!" in a poem, unconsciously echoing God's laughter in "Channel Firing," he wrote beside it, "Too Hardy a laugh."

I don't know if I ever wrote a poem that he found successful while I was his student, but he let me know that he thought I had what it took to be a writer and told me when I graduated that if I stopped writing at any time for any reason in the next ten years, the muses should strike me deaf, dumb, and blind. It was a powerful admonition. Eight years later I dedicated my first book to him.

For an eighteen-year-old poet in 1970 the University of California at Santa Cruz was an exciting place to be. George Hitchcock had been invited to teach there at College V, the arts college, by the provost, James B. Hall. I was enrolled at College V, having no idea what to expect except redwoods. Like a lot of other Southern California students, I just wanted to get out of the L.A. Basin.

Hitchcock had been editing the little poetry magazine *kayak* for about six years when he came to Santa Cruz to teach. His press had been publishing books for half that time. My classmates from the Bay Area knew about him. One of them even had copies of some of Hitchcock's own beautiful, limited-edition books of poems, *Poems & Prints* and *The Dolphin with the Revolver in Its Teeth*. At a welcoming party at the home of one of the faculty who lived on campus, I found a copy of his latest book, *A Ship of Bells*, and read it curiously. I knew nothing about surrealism, at least as practiced by Hitchcock. I sat thinking what I could do if I could make poems with such images.

I discovered his magazine before I ever met Hitchcock himself. The bookstore had recent issues of *kayak* for sale. On my own I had already found the work of Philip Levine and W. S. Merwin, Charles Simic and James Tate, and *kayak* had new poems by them. There were also poems by Margaret Atwood and Nancy Willard, John Haines and Vern Rutsala, whom I had never heard of, but who were writing marvelous things. There were strange and hilarious letters to the editor. Polemical reviews. And throughout, prints of people in Victorian dress involved in activities, like measuring a skull with calipers or simply standing in their underwear, that contrasted provocatively with the poems.

One night early in the school year a group of us who were taking a poetry writing class were invited to Hitchcock's house in Bonny Doon to read our work aloud and to meet other poets. Hitchcock had the bearing of an actor who could play Lear or Pozzo and seemed amused by the charcoal resonance of his own baritone voice. I think he was taller than anyone else that evening, with long gray hair that covered his ears, and a light in his blue eyes that was old-fashioned merriment. There were some very sharp, very witty young people present, and their remarks and poems delighted him. His house was full of books. On a coffee table where he had been working was a galley proof of Philip Levine's *Red Dust,* which kayak press would soon publish. We were allowed to roam around, even into his workroom in the back, and saw the mock-ups for the next issue of *kayak.* Outside the house was surrounded by redwoods, bay laurel, and madrone, and a stream ran past. Inside Hitchcock presided indulgently over our reading. I left with a borrowed copy of Mark Strand's *Darker,* another discovery. I began to think of George Hitchcock as the man who lived in the House of Poetry.

Over the next four years I took a couple of poetry writing classes with George and a course on George Bernard Shaw. But most important and most fortunate for me was watching him and eventually helping him to edit *kayak.* In one of George's poetry writing classes I met Robert McDowell, who had a sophisticated gift for writing in a bitterly funny yet lyrical surrealist style that George encouraged in his students. I could never write that way, and I admired McDowell's ability to do something I could not. We became friends, and the two of us began to spend as much time around George as we could and as he would permit.

He allowed us to go through the enormous number of manuscripts that were submitted weekly to *kayak.* It was understood that we knew his taste in poetry and that we were to look for things that might please him. I found increasingly that George and I did not agree about poetry. He shared Robert Bly's view of W. H. Auden, and I held Auden's view of Bly. When I tried to find common ground with him, he told me it was more interesting to talk about where and why we disagreed. I developed my own preferences and honed my critical skills in argument with George. Subsequently he published my first essays and book reviews in *kayak*.

By the time we graduated from college, Robert McDowell and I were devoted to George and his companion Marjorie Simon. Their house on Ocean View Avenue was a mecca for writers and poetry lovers. My wife Amy and I were married there, in the House of Poetry, on December 28, 1974.

The Reaper

After college, Amy and I moved to Iowa City where I attended the Writers' Workshop. Robert McDowell entered the M.F.A. program at Columbia. I studied with Donald Justice and Charles Wright. Robert studied with Richard Eberhart and William Jay Smith. When we left graduate school we began to find ourselves increasingly at odds with the general drift of contemporary poetry. Robert had been doing a good deal of experimentation with traditional forms. I was writing a kind of autobiographical narrative verse. The small, imagistic lyric that focused on the poet's private feelings seemed exhausted, and it looked as if American poetry was headed in the direction of looser, often abstract, self-referential meditation, in the style of Ashbery. Robert and I knew we didn't fit in with any of this.

In 1980 circumstances brought us within close proximity for the first time since college. Robert was teaching at Indiana State University, Evansville (now the University of Southern Indiana), and I was at Murray State University, in Murray, Kentucky. The two places were about three hours apart by car. We felt isolated, though we were lucky to have jobs. We were angry because we didn't see anyone else writing or praising the kind of poems we were writing or wanted to write. Robert had recently attended a poetry symposium called "After the Flood" at the Folger Shakespeare Library in Washington, D.C., and listened to Harold Bloom, Donald Davie, John Hollander, Richard Howard, Marjorie Perloff, and Stanley Plumly give papers on the state of the art. He didn't like anything he heard and took copious notes.

He shared his notes with me, and I didn't like it either. We decided to collaborate on a rebuttal.

We had written collaborations in college, usually parodies, but for George Hitchcock's class on George Bernard Shaw, we had contrived a terrible play "in the Shavian manner" that read more like a bad script for *Columbo*. Still, each of us had a good sense of how the other thought, and we knew how to write a sentence together.

Then, Robert proposed that we do more than write a rebuttal, that we start a magazine. He had pitched the idea of a literary magazine to his dean, who liked it and said he would provide access to the school's printing and binding services and some financial backing. My tendency in the face of most radical departures that I haven't thought of myself is to say, "No." Robert has always been ready to take a risk. He drew a parallel between *kayak* and what he envisioned: we would edit and publish a magazine devoted to our views of what poetry should be. Those views were not particularly clear, except that we were against the going trend. We would excite and anger people. We would castigate our enemies. We would publish our friends. Robert has a depth of Irish persuasion and a Teutonic drive that for all my skepticism and dourness I find hard to resist. I agreed to start a magazine.

We called it *The Reaper* and imagined the grim figure as a symbol of change as much as death. Along with an essay on "After the Flood," we wrote a manifesto, "Where *The Reaper* Stands," for the first issue:

> *The Reaper* is the great deleter, the one who determines when the story ends. Most contemporary poets have forgotten him. Navel gazers and mannerists, their time is running out. Their poems, too long even when they are short, full of embarrassing lines that "context" is supposed to justify, confirm the suspicion that our poets just aren't listening to their language anymore. Editors and critics aren't listening much, either. Despite their best red-faced efforts, their favorite gods—inaccuracy, bathos, sentimentality, posturing, evasion—wither at the sound of *The Reaper*'s whetstone singing. . . .
> *The Reaper* maintains that both the accurate image and the narrative line, two determining factors of the poem's shapeli-

ness, have been keenly honed and kept sharp by the poets included here, whereas many of their counterparts, forgetting these necessities, have wandered into a formless swamp where only the skunk cabbage of solipsistic meditation breeds, with its cloying flowers.

It is *The Reaper*'s ultimate aim to drain the bog of American writing by providing a format for poems and stories that take chances and make squeamish the editors of most other literary magazines with more fashionable "tastes." . . .

The poems collected here in issue number one, unmannered, tell stories *which their imagery serves*. Their authors know when to stop, which acknowledges the role of *The Reaper*. They believe, in fact, in death, which gives us only so much time to tell our story, defining its necessity and making the choice of imagery urgent.

Do contemporary writers think they can wander the marshland forever? *The Reaper*'s scythe is already whispering at their heels!

After she read our manifesto, whenever *The Reaper* was mentioned, Amy would say "Pffft! Pffft!" for his whispering scythe. Another friend warned us that after you drain a marsh, all you are left with is mud.

In the first issue of *The Reaper,* we didn't really have the kind of poem we described in our statement. But it became clear to us that we were interested in narrative poetry. It took several issues before we started finding and publishing the sort of narrative poems we began to describe in our essays. By the time we finished doing the magazine in 1989, we had published major narrative poems by many younger poets who were working in the form, including Rita Dove, Garrett Hongo, Andrew Hudgins, Sydney Lea, Mary Swander, and Chase Twichell. Our essays, always written from the point of view of our persona, The Reaper, included an evaluation of the unfortunate influence of Wallace Stevens, an appraisal of Robert Frost as America's greatest narrative poet, "How to Write a Narrative Poem: A Reaper Checklist," and "*The Reaper*'s Non-negotiable Demands." We also made up an exchange of letters between Homer and Dante on the art of epic and an interview with a highly successful po-biz couple, Sean Dough and Jean Doh. Many of the cranky letters to the editor we wrote ourselves. We managed to infuriate all of the people we had hoped to and more. We had a blast.

We tried not to take ourselves too seriously, but our conversations about the role of narrative in poetry, the necessity that a poem have some story to tell and that poems be about other characters besides the poet, led us both to experiment with ways of telling a story in a poem. The result for Robert was his first collection of poetry, *Quiet Money*, published by Holt in 1987. Its title poem tells the moving and remarkable story of a bootlegger who flies the Atlantic solo before Lindbergh and later helps during the investigation into the Lindbergh baby's kidnapping. My own collection of narrative experiments, *The Black Riviera*, was published in 1990 and dedicated to Robert.

The Reaper died in 1989, but its healthy offspring, Story Line Press, lives on. In 1985 the Nicholas Roerich Museum in New York City proposed that we begin a poetry series that they would fund. From that beginning Story Line Press has gone on with Robert as editor and publisher to do more than one hundred titles in poetry, fiction, nonfiction, drama, and translation.

Children

Many of the poems in my first four books are about childhood, either my own or my parents' or my grandparents'. They are usually narratives and based on stories I have been told or I have told myself. When I write about my own children, I have the feeling that I am writing about strangers whose stories I can only guess at, countries with secret histories. My sense of childhood's power and ultimate secrecy, which has always been strong, has been increased by recent events in my mother's life.

My mother, Bo Dee, was born in Harlingen, Texas. Her name is a respelling of Bodie, her mother's maiden name. One of her earliest memories is of a Mexican woman in her mother's kitchen patting dough between her hands to make tortillas. Another, after her parents moved to California, is of taking the bus with her mother across country to Wiggins, Mississippi, to visit her grandparents, Alonso and Allie Bodie. Her clearest childhood memory is of her parents' divorce. Four years old she sits on the running board of her father's Hudson and asks him why he has to leave. She also recalls a day, after her parents were divorced, when her father came to pick her up at school. She is certain that he was not supposed to do that. He took her on a long outing and introduced her to the woman who would become her stepmother. Though her own mother never commented on the incident, my mother is sure that her father kidnapped her.

In 1983, after thirty-three years of marriage, my father left my mother. Recently we discovered that she had been suffering for many years from an excess of cranial fluid, a condition known clinically as normal pressure hydrocephalis (NPH). It is an insidious disease that gradually results in incontinence, short-term memory loss, and loss of balance. An operation in 1992 restored some of her faculties, but the NPH and her grief have undermined her physically and psychologically. It is rare that she speaks of any event later than our three years in Scotland. She often revisits her four-year-old self on the running board of her father's car, as he prepares to leave his wife and his daughter.

After spending most of her life on the West Coast, my mother now lives in Nashville, Tennessee, where Amy and I moved with our two children in 1983 when I took a teaching position at Vanderbilt University. Since my mother prefers to talk about what for me is the distant past, when we are together I am put in touch again and again with events from my own childhood. When I was growing up in Redondo, my family's great aid to memory was that my father, who was an excellent amateur photographer, had an extensive slide and film collection of places we had lived and traveled. I know this kept my memory of Scotland and Europe sharp and clear. Now that I no longer have access to those pictures (my father lives in California), my mother's dwelling on the past often serves the same purpose. Her memory will suddenly project an image or a story that brings me or my sisters back as children, sharply, clearly, and, because of her deep depression, painfully.

I know that in raising our children we repeat what our parents did in raising us. Our first child, Claire Marie, was born May 15, 1980, in Mission Viejo, California, when I was teaching as a guest lecturer at the University of California, Irvine. At the end of that year, we moved to Kentucky, where I took a job at Murray State University. Though totally coincidental, still this move in some ways parallels in reverse my parents' move from Kentucky, where I was born, back to California. Our second, Zoë Anne, was born December 16, 1982, in Murray. Amy has often taken the girls with her to Colorado where her mother now lives, and Claire and Zoë have both gone to visit their grandmother there alone, just as when she was growing up, Amy would travel by herself to Colorado to spend summers with her grandparents in Greeley. In 1989 I directed Vanderbilt's junior year abroad program in England at the University of Leeds. Claire and Zoë spent a year in English schools and became friends with the four wonderful children who lived next door. They came home to America sounding like a pair of Yorkshire lasses. Before we went to England, I prepared the children by reading to them from a collection of letters that my father had sent to his sister between 1958 and 1961, while we lived in Scotland. I was creating a parallel between my childhood and my children's.

Claire and Zoë have the good fortune to have a mother who is a superb musician, a lyric coloratura with a heartbreaking voice, who has made music a central part of their lives. Claire plays the piano, and Zoë is a violinist in the Nashville Youth Repertory Orchestra. They are both readers and are able to carry on poised, intelligent conversations with adults. At the same time, our daughters, as the poet James Wright would say, are their own secrets. At present, those secrets have to do with being teenagers. And we can only guess at them, as we overhear phone conversations or the emanations from their Walkmen. Because of their parents' nostalgia for California, they seem to think of themselves as Californians. Maybe they will be someday. Pulling up roots and crossing the continent, even crossing the ocean, is a family tradition. But for now they are growing up in Nashville, Tennessee. They are Southerners.

Amy and I have spoken frankly about my mother in the children's presence, perhaps too frankly. When we pick up their Grandmother Bo Dee for church on Sunday morning, they look at her with concern and pity. I have seen it in their faces. My mother is always delighted to see her granddaughters. She takes her seat in the car and begins almost at once to reminisce for them about Scotland or her own childhood memories of the South, in Harlingen or Wiggins. I think she will be an important part of Claire and Zoë's memory of childhood.

Faith

One evening in early November 1973, during my senior year at UC Santa Cruz, I was on the phone to Robert McDowell, when a person I had never met entered the house where I lived with a couple who were also students. She had come by to pick up the woman, who was making costumes for a student production of *Jacques Brel Is Alive and Well and Living in Paris.* I remember that Robert asked what was wrong, because I had stopped talking.

The stranger was Amy Kane, one of the stars of the production. We had moved in the same circles in college for three years without meeting. I attended her first performance and made a point of introducing myself afterwards backstage. I attended the rest of the performances, too. Years later, when she was asked by an interviewer why she finally agreed to go out with me, she said, "I couldn't resist such devotion."

I don't believe we are destined to find our lifemate. I know too many people who never have. Maybe we only meet them if we're lucky, and perhaps for some, like my parents, it is not lucky in the end. But I believe when Amy Kane walked into that student house that night and I saw her and stopped talking, that I had an experience of the kind of luck that W. H. Auden called grace. Not to put too fine a theological point on it, I believe when I met Amy that something greater than myself but also deep within me said, "You have been given a gift."

Amy left college to come with me to graduate school. In Iowa City she worked as a waitress and in social services to support us. She also started taking lessons in classical voice. When I was appointed to my first teaching job at Indiana State University in Evansville, she entered the University of Evansville on a scholarship and earned a B.A. in music. In 1978 when I received a National Endowment for the Arts grant in poetry and quit my job at Evansville, we went to live in Italy where Amy studied singing at the Conservatorio Morlacchi in Perugia. Today she sings opera, oratorio, and gives solo recitals throughout the United States and England.

In 1978 I had not been in a church for nearly seven years and had no interest at all in going to one. I nursed my father's bitter experience in Redondo like a grudge. Amy and I were living in Todi, in Umbria, and she had joined *il Coro di Todi,* which sang regularly in the region's churches. One Sunday when Amy was singing with *il Coro* at San Fortunato, the Franciscan church in the town, I attended. I had been reading Henry Adams's *Mont San Michel and Chartres* and been moved by his depiction of how medieval Christians gathered in their churches, these great centers of power, to worship the Virgin. I realized on that Sunday that I was standing among many of the citizens of the town, almost as Adams imagined them—there were no pews—and listening to them respond at places in the service, like the Gloria Patri and the Doxology, that I recognized from my own upbringing. It began to occur to me at an inarticulate level that in my estrangement from the church and from God I was denying an essential part of myself.

In 1986 we had been in Nashville three years. I had tenure, and Amy had begun teaching voice at Vanderbilt's music school. The girls had been attending the church where Amy sang in the choir, and she decided that it was time we all started going to church someplace together. Her decision was not religious; it had everything to do with our family. But for me it was a religious decision. It required admitting to myself that I still had a faith, complicated not only by what had happened to my father but, after my parents' divorce, by what my father had done to my mother. We decided to go together to a church in my denomination.

And things have become even more interesting and complicated in the intervening years. Amy is Jewish but was raised with very little sense of her religion. She and our daughter Zoë have joined the Reformed Temple in Nashville. Amy sings in the Temple choir. We are all still members of Vine Street Christian Church, but usually only my daughter Claire, who has been baptized, my mother, and I attend. Amy also sings in the choir at

Christ Church Episcopal. On Sunday morning, when Zoë goes to Hebrew school, we head in several ecumenical directions.

As an epigraph to *The Rote Walker* I quoted two lines from John Logan's poem "The Spring of the Thief": "When we speak of God, / Is it God we speak of?" I used to say flippantly that the answer to that profound question was "Yes and no." I no longer think the answer is flippant. It is just as profound as the question. When I met Amy Kane I began, without knowing it, a return to faith, not the faith of my fathers, exactly, but a faith *in* fathers— and mothers, too, for that matter. It was a faith in custom and culture, the society that made me who I am, and the family that loved me. And it was a recognition that there was something greater behind these things.

In a little autograph book I owned as a child in Scotland and which I still have, my father wrote, from Micah 6:8: "And what does the Lord require of you but to do justice, and to love kindness and to walk humbly with your God?" That passage has never failed to move me, even when I did not know who my God was. At this point in my life, with the help and love of my wife and children, I am finding out.